Empowered Girls

Empowered Girls

A Girl's Guide to Positive Activism,
Volunteering, and Philanthropy

Frances A. Karnes &
Kristen R. Stephens

Graphic Production Libby Goolsby

ISBN 1-59363-163-4
    Library of Congress Cataloging-in-Publication Data

Karnes, Frances A.
    Empowered girls : a girl's guide to positive activism, volunteering,
and philanthropy / Frances A. Karnes & Kristen R. Stephens.
      p. cm.
    ISBN 1-59363-163-4 (pbk.)
    1. Girl volunteers—United States—Juvenile literature. 2. Young
volunteers in social service—United States—Case studies—Juvenile
literature. 3. Young volunteers in community development—United
States—Case studies—Juvenile literature. 4. Voluntarism—United
States—Case studies—Juvenile literature. 5. Social action—United
States—Case studies—Juvenile literature. 6. Charity organization
—United States—Case studies—Juvenile literature.   I. Stephens,
Kristen R. II. Title.
HN90.V64K36 2006
361.3'7'083520973--dc22
                                                    2005018381

At the time of this book's publication, all facts and figures cited are the most current available; all telephone numbers, addresses, and Web site URLs are accurate
and active; all publications, organizations, Web sites, and other resources exist as
described in this book; and all have been verified. The authors and Prufrock Press
make no warranty or guarantee concerning the information and materials given
out by organizations or content found at Web sites, and we are not responsible
for any changes that occur after this book's publication. If you find an error or
believe that a resource listed here is not as described, please contact Prufrock
Press.

PRUFROCK PRESS, INC.
P.O. Box 8813
Waco, TX 76714-8813
Phone: (800) 998-2208
Fax: (800) 240-0333
http://www.prufrock.com

Dedication

This book is dedicated to Mary Ryan and Emma Karnes,
and to all the charitable girls and young women
who make our towns, cities, states, and nation
better places for all citizens.

Contents

*"How wonderful is it
that nobody need wait a single moment
before starting to improve the world."*

—Anne Frank

Acknowledgments

Many persons have contributed to the completion of this publication. Our special thanks are extended to the girls and young women who contributed their stories and who serve as outstanding role models for charitable endeavors. To the adults who provided inspirational quotes we extend our gratitude.

In order to locate the empowered girls to contribute their stories, announcements regarding the book were distributed through several channels: state educational associations and consultants, organizations for girls, and school districts. To all the adults who assisted in locating empowered girls, please know how grateful we are.

Several people were helpful in the production of the manuscript. The staff at the Frances A. Karnes Center for Gifted Studies has been supportive in many ways. The administrators at The University of Southern Mississippi and at the Duke University Talent Identification Program have been very supportive of our publication's production. Special recognition is extended to our publisher for the encouragement and support of this book.

Our families deserve special acknowledgement for their love and encouragement. Ray, John, Leighanne, Mary Ryan, John Morris, and Emma Karnes; Rich, Jack, and David Kozak; Alan and Dorothy Stephens have given us their support. The special guidance of Christopher J. Karnes and Karen and David Stephens will always be with us throughout our lives.

Part 1: Introduction

> *"Every individual matters.*
> *Every individual has a role to play.*
> *Every individual makes a difference."*
> —Dr. Jane Goodall

Positive activism, volunteering, and philanthropy should not be concepts limited to adults. Currently, there is an interest in raising a new generation of children and youth who act upon larger societal needs. Girls typically have a natural willingness to help others. If this trait is nurtured, girls may be more likely to make a difference in their community.

A 2000 survey found that 27% of high school girls participate in service or volunteer groups through school as opposed to 18% of boys. While 86% of teenagers feel it is important for corporations to contribute to charity, 60% of girls and 40% of boys are actually involved in any philanthropic activity (Raymond, 2002).

Why should you get involved?

Learning to give, whether through contributing time or money, is a valuable skill to possess, as it enhances your self-concept and sense of social responsibility. Your academic skills can also be strengthened by engaging in critical thinking as you develop and implement solutions to the problems and needs around you. Contributing also makes you feel

1

good and provides a sense of empowerment pertaining to something in which you really believe.

In addition to the personal benefits you will receive from getting involved, other individuals and organizations will benefit as well. For example, almost every organization lacks the resources, both financial and human, that are needed in order to carry out their established goals. *You* can help them achieve their goals through charitable gifts, your time, or money.

How do you get involved?

If you are not sure at this point what it is you would like to do, take some time to look around your school and community, watch the news, read your local paper, surf the Internet. Browsing these areas can give you an idea of what's out there and what causes need action.

You can follow the ACT Model to help you get involved. There are basically three steps in this model: Ask, Choose, and Tackle (ACT). Each step is detailed below.

Step 1: Ask

Step 1 involves *asking* yourself and others some questions that will assist in selecting a cause. For example:
- What identified problems concern me the most?
- What are my interests? (i.e., animals, children, the poor, the environment)
- What talent or skills do I have to offer?
- How much time or money do I have to commit?
- What exactly do I want to do? (volunteer, donate money, start a new project to address a problem)
- Will I enjoy this type of service?

Step 2: Choose

After you have selected your cause, it is time to *choose* how you want to help. List all your ideas for resolving the selected problem or issue. Be creative and list *all* possible solutions. After you have generated 10 or more resolutions, rank your ideas. You may even want to create a rubric to evaluate each idea. Some questions you may want to consider in the evaluation process include:

- Does this solution address the "real" problem?
- How feasible is this solution?
- Will this solution have the desired impact?

Step 3: Tackle

After selecting the proposed solution, it is time to take action and *tackle* that problem! It is a good idea to develop a plan for implementing your great idea. Questions that may need to be considered during this step include:

- Will I need additional funding?
- Will I need the help of friends and family members?
- What other resources will be necessary?

Finding Funding

Sometimes, money is needed to get your idea or project off the ground. There are many methods for obtaining the funds necessary, but it can be time-consuming, so plan accordingly. If a small amount of money is needed, a creative fund-raiser may be the best option. Auctions, a-thons, flower sales, raffles, and car washes are just a few ideas. You can also ask your friends and family for donations toward your project through direct phone or letter solicitation. If the project requires a large amount of money, a grant proposal may be a more suitable approach. Call your mayor's office for groups funding projects for youth. Youth Acton Net (http://www.youthactionnet.org/toolkit.php) provides advice and ideas on how to fund your project and is worth checking out. Following are a few organizations that provide money to youth for worthwhile projects.

Ellen Dougherty Activist Fund
http://www.openmeadows.org/special.htm
Provides grants of up to $2,000 to women 19 and under who propose to develop and lead projects focused on activism and social change. The application deadlines are February 15 and August 15 of each year.

David Brower Youth Awards
http://www.earthisland.org
Every year, six outstanding young environmental leaders from the United States and Puerto Rico receive this award from Earth Island Institute. Each are awarded a $3,000 cash prize, a trip to Yosemite National Park, local and national media exposure, and access to key mentors and organizational resources to further their work.

YouthActionNet Awards
http://www.youthactionnet.org/yan_awards
Youth Action Net offers $500 awards for young people who are working on projects that support social change and are helping to connect youth with their local communities.

Youth As Resources
http://www.yar.org
Encourages youth-led and youth-designed community projects. They help young people from ages 5 to 21 find funding sources and adult assistance within their communities to get their projects going.

Do Something
http://www.dosomething.org
Awards grants of $500 to students in the Do Something Network who have project ideas to help their communities.

The Gloria Barron Prize for Young Heroes
http://www.barronprize.org
Awards $2,000 to young people (ages 8–18) from diverse backgrounds who have organized and led an extraordinary service activity to benefit other people, animals, or the planet.

Youth Venture
http://www.youthventure.org
Offers up to $1,000 in start-up funds and all the support necessary to launch your own civic-minded organization, club, or business.

Youth Noise
http://www.youthnoise.com
Offers grants up to $1,000 to support youth-led projects designed to improve members' communities or schools.

Joining an Existing Project
You can either start your own project using the ACT Model or you can join an existing program that shares your mission and interests. There are a multitude of organizations that need enthusiastic and dedicated individuals to assist in reaching their goals. Some resources for locating such programs follow.

Corporation for National and Community Service
http://www.nationalservice.org
Connects Americans of all ages and backgrounds with opportunities to give back to their communities and their nation through voluntary service.

Greenpeace
http://www.greenpeace.org
Volunteer opportunities for those interested in helping protect the planet.

Idealist Kids and Teens
http://www.idealist.org/kt
Helps people find the resources and support they need to help themselves and their communities.

Just for Kids
http://www.volunteerhouston.org/kids
Volunteer Houston has put together this site filled with information on topics such as What's Hot for Kids, 10 Good Reasons for Kids to Volunteer, Ideas for Self Starters, and Useful and Fun Links.

Kids Can Make A Difference
http://www.kidscanmakeadifference.org
An educational program for middle and high school students focusing on hunger and poverty.

Kids Care Clubs
http://www.kidscare.org
Visit this site to learn how you can start your own club and see what other kids are doing.

National Wildlife Federation
http://www.nwf.org/kids
The nation's largest member-supported conservation group, uniting individuals, organizations, businesses, and government to protect wildlife, wild places, and the environment.

Network for Good
http://www.networkforgood.org
Explore volunteering opportunities, learn how to start a nonprofit, and see a list of resources on working in the nonprofit sector.

Points of Light Foundation
http://www.pointsoflight.org
The Foundation's mission is to engage more people more effectively in volunteer community service to help solve serious social problems.

SERVEnet.org
http://www.servenet.org
Offers service and volunteering opportunities. Users can enter their zip code, city, state, skills, interests, and availability and be matched with organizations needing help.

VolunteerMatch
http://www.volunteermatch.org
Connecting volunteers with nearly 25,000 community service organizations around the U.S.

Youth Service America
http://www.ysa.org
A resource center and the premier alliance of more than 300 organizations committed to increasing the quantity and quality of volunteer opportunities for young Americans (ages 5–25) to serve locally, nationally, and globally.

Part 2: Positive Activism

"Never doubt that a small group of thoughtful, committed citizens can change the world; indeed, it's the only thing that ever has."

—Margaret Mead

What is positive activism?

Positive activism involves taking action in support of a cause in which you believe. You can work alone or organize with others. All you need is the time, energy, and will to make a difference and initiate change. *Positive* activism should be distinguished from other forms of activism that may be associated with confrontation.

How do I get started?

Change is not easy, but here are a few tips that can assist you in getting started.

- **Research.** Make certain that you know all the ins and outs of the issue. Are there any policies, rules, or laws that come into play? Is change possible?
- **Find out who's in charge.** Who are the decision-makers you will need to convince to initiate the proposed change? Present your case to those who have the power to put your ideas into action.
- **Get Support.** Who else would be interested in the proposed initiative? What individuals would benefit from your idea? Get them on board!

- **Stay positive.** Work toward a resolution that is agreeable to everyone involved. Be willing to listen and understand the other positions regarding the issue.
- **Start with a phone-call or letter.** You may be surprised that your idea or suggestion is considered and implemented right away—eliminating the need for a public campaign.

What are some strategies that positive activists use?

There are a variety of methods and means used by positive activists to make others aware of their efforts and to initiate grassroots change.

Petitions can be used to gain public support and often have a powerful impact on decision makers. They should clearly and concisely outline your case and make a call for action. Let the local media know the date and time you plan to deliver the petition to the "decision-making" recipient. This will further help to spread the word about your cause.

Letters to the editor of newspapers and to elected officials can also be valuable tools for the positive activist. Keep your letter clear, polite, and to the point. Remember that your goal is to *influence*, not *insult* the reader. Enlist others to join in your letter-writing campaign. Be sure to coordinate your efforts. A barrage of letters received over the course of a few weeks will really get an official's attention.

If letter writing and petitions do not work as intended, you can *attend public meetings* and make your presence known. This direct approach will certainly get you noticed. It is advised that you try to get an appointment to address the committee or board. If they do not let you speak the first time, continue to attend their meetings until you are allowed to be heard.

Additional Tips

Research, research, research! Become an expert on your issue.

- Why tackle the issue solo? Organize a school or community meeting to get other people interested and involved in your cause.
- Look for existing coalitions with similar goals as your group and ask to join.
- Tell everyone you know about your cause and ask them to spread the word. This can be accomplished through word-of-mouth, letters, newsletters, e-mails, listservs, phone trees, and Web pages.
- Know your local media. Develop a press kit that details your cause.
- Monitor and evaluate progress toward your goals.
- Stay focused and remember persistence can pay off.

" The great end of life is not knowledge but action. "
—Thomas Henry Huxley

Web Sites

At The Table
http://www.atthetable.org
Provides resources and information about how to involve young people in decision making.

Constitutional Rights Foundation
http://www.crf-usa.org
Educates America's young people about the importance of civic participation in a democratic society.

Global Youth Action Network
http://www.youthlink.org
A growing collaboration among youth and youth organizations that are committed to uniting their efforts to improve our world.

Kids Can Make A Difference
http://www.kidscanmakeadifference.org
Focuses on the root causes of hunger and poverty, the people most affected, solutions, and how students can help.

Project 540
http://www.project540.org
Gives students nationwide the opportunity to talk about issues that matter to them and to turn these conversations into real school and community change.

What Kids Can Do
http://www.whatkidscando.org
Documents the value of young people working with teachers and other adults on projects that combine powerful learning with public purpose.

Wiretap
http://www.wiretapmag.org
An independent information source by and for socially conscious youth.

Youth Action Network
http://www.youthactionnetwork.org
Dedicated to helping youth become more informed and actively involved in order to move toward a just and sustainable society.

Youth Activism
http://www.youthactivism.com
Encourages young people to speak up and pursue lasting solutions to problems they care about.

The Youth Empowerment Center
http://www.youthec.org
Represents the development of young people creating new organizations, institutions, and intermediaries that meet the needs of their constituencies and communities.

Youth in Action
http://www.youthlink.org/us
Provides support and recognition for the voices, ideas, and positive solutions of youth.

"*You must be the change you wish to see in the world.***"**
—Mahatma Gandhi

Books

Avakian, M. (2000). *Reformers: Activists, educators, religious leaders*. Austin, TX: Raintree.

Campolo, A., Rice, W., & McNabb, B. (1985). *Ideas for social action*. Grand Rapids, MI: Zondervan.

Rappaport, H. (2001). *Women social reformers: A biographical dictionary*. Santa Barbara, CA: ABC-CLIO.

Rusch, E. (2002). *Generation fix: Young ideas for a better world*. Hillsboro, OR: Beyond Words.

Schneider, D. J. (1993). *American women in the Progressive Era, 1900–1920*. New York: Facts on File.

> **"***It's amazing what one can do when one doesn't know what one can do.***"**
> —Garfield the Cat

Organizations

Alliance for Justice
11 Dupont Circle NW
2nd Floor
Washington, DC 20036
Phone: (202) 822-6070; Fax: (202) 822-6068
E-mail: Alliance@afj.org
http://www.allianceforjustice.org
Works to advance the cause of justice for all Americans, strengthen the public interest in the community's ability to influence public policy, and foster the next generation of advocates.

Amnesty International
322 8th Ave.
New York, NY 10001
Phone: (212) 807-8400; Fax: (212) 463-9193
E-mail: admin-us@aiusa.org
http://www.amnesty.org
A worldwide campaigning movement that works to promote internationally recognized human rights.

Center for Community Change
1000 Wisconsin Ave. NW
Washington, DC 20007
Phone: (202) 342-0567; Fax: (202) 333-5462
E-mail: info@communitychange.org
http://www.communitychange.org
Nationally recognized for its work helping people build organizations and create better communities and policies.

JustAct
333 Valencia St., Ste. 325
San Francisco, CA 94103
Phone: (415) 431-4204; Fax: (415) 431-5953
E-mail: info@justact.org
http://www.justact.org
Promotes youth leadership and action for global justice.

National Youth Rights Association
P.O. Box 5882, NW
Washington DC, 20016
E-mail: info@youthrights.org
http://www.youthrights.org
Dedicated to defending the civil and human rights of young people in the United States.

Sierra Club
85 Second St., 2nd Floor
San Francisco, CA 94105
Phone: (415) 977-5500; Fax: (415) 977-5799
E-mail: information@sierraclub.org
http://www.sierraclub.org
America's oldest, largest, and most influential grassroots environmental organization.

Part 3: Volunteering and Community Service

"Giving back is a part of participating.
Helping others merely mirrors
what so many have done to help us.
And we are where we are today not just through our own
efforts, but because of the path blazed by those
who have gone before us."

—Cathleen Black

What is volunteering and community service?

If you do not have the money to give toward a cause, you can always donate your time. Volunteering and community service involve offering some of your time and skills to help. Examples of volunteering and community service can include tutoring, community clean-ups, working in a soup kitchen, or assisting at an animal shelter. Many grassroots organizations depend on volunteers to meet their goals. Remember, it is unlikely that you will be *asked* to volunteer—you must take the initiative and seek out opportunities to help on your own.

Why volunteer?

Helping others will make you feel good and help you gain a broader perspective of the world through experiential learning. You can contribute your knowledge, talents, ideas and time to help improve your community, state, the nation, or even the world! It also looks good on college applications—but this should not be your main reason for volunteering. Volunteering is a commitment. Be certain that you are willing to devote the time asked of you. Some volunteering opportunities may be one-day projects, while others are ongoing. In addition, you can either join an existing effort or create your own project in which to volunteer your time.

There are many things you can learn through volunteering and community service. For example:

- **Responsibility.** By volunteering, you are making and keeping a commitment; therefore, you gain a better sense of time management.
- **Sacrifice**. You learn that there are more important issues than your own immediate needs.
- **Tolerance.** You will have the opportunity to work with people of different backgrounds who share common values.
- **Empowerment**. You learn that you can have an impact on someone or something.
- **Teamwork**. You can learn effective methods for working with others, assume leadership roles, and set goals. All of these skills will be helpful in any future career.

What opportunities are out there, and how do I find them?

There are many volunteering opportunities. In deciding what you would like to do, think about what interests you. Is it the environment? Children? Health? Poverty? Animal welfare? Find an opportunity that suits your interests and skills. Select something you will enjoy. A great place to start looking for opportunities is Volunteer Match (http://www.volunteermatch.org). You can search for volunteer opportunities by zip code at their Web site.

"Everyone can be great because anyone can serve.
You don't have to have a college degree to serve.
You don't even have to make your subject
and your verb agree to serve ...
You only need a heart full of grace.
A soul generated by love."

—Martin Luther King, Jr.

Web Sites

**e-Volunteerism Online Journal
of the Volunteer Community**
http://www.e-volunteerism.com
An electronic journal for volunteers.

Idealist.org
http://www.idealist.org/
Helps people find resources and support they need to help themselves and their community.

**Learning in Deed: Making a Difference
Through Service-Learning**
http://www.learningindeed.org
Service-learning information source.

National Service-Learning Clearinghouse
http://www.servicelearning.org
Includes resources on service-learning.

Network for the Good
http://www.networkforgood.org
Dedicated to using the Web to help people get more involved in their communities.

Peace Corp Kids World
http://www.peacecorps.gov/kids
Explains what it means to make a difference and talks about becoming a Peace Corp volunteer.

**Points of Light Foundation and Volunteer Center
National Network**
http://www.pointsoflight.org
Promotes volunteerism.

The Virtual Volunteering Project
http://www.serviceleader.org/vv/vonline4.html
Provides Web sites and information on volunteering.

Volunteering England
http://www.volunteering.org.uk
Advice and information on volunteering.

Volunteer Management
http://www.energizeinc.com
Features sources and books on volunteerism.

Volunteerism–Suite101.com
http://www.suite101.com/welcome.cfm/volunteerism
Provides discussions, articles, and links about volunteerism.

Youth Service America
http://www.ysa.org
Resource center provides youth with information to help them serve.

Zoom Into Action
http://pbskids.org/zoom/action
Multimedia campaign that promotes kids to volunteer.

<blockquote>"Make yourself necessary to someone."
—Ralph Waldo Emerson</blockquote>

Books

Case, S., & Cornforth, F. (1995). *Hands-on service ideas for youth groups.* Loveland, CO: Group.

DeGeronimo, T. (1995). *A student's guide to volunteering.* Franklin Lakes, NJ: Career Press.

Duper, L. L. (1996). *160 ways to help the world: Community service projects for young people.* New York: Facts on File.

Erlbach, A. (1998). *The kids' volunteering book.* Minneapolis: Lerner.

Goodman, A. (1994). *The big help book: 365 ways you can make a difference by volunteering.* New York: Pocket Books.

Gralla, P. (2001). *Complete idiot's guide to volunteering for teens.* Indianapolis: Pearson Education.

Hovanec, E. M. (1999). *Get involved!: A girl's guide to volunteering.* New York: Rosen.

Isler, C. (2000). *Volunteering to help in your neighborhood.* New York: Scholastic Library.

Isler, C. (2000). *Volunteering to help with animals.* New York: Scholastic Library.

Karnes, F. A., & Beane, S. M. (1993). *Girls and young women leading the way: 20 true stories about leadership.* Minneapolis: Free Spirit.

Karnes, F. A., & Beane, S. M. (1995). *Leadership for students: A practical guide for ages 8–18.* Waco, TX: Prufrock Press.

Klee, S. (2000). *Volunteering for a political campaign.* New York: Scholastic Library.

Lewis, B. (1995). *The kid's guide to service projects: Over 500 service ideas for young people who want to make a difference.* Minneapolis: Free Spirit.

Murdico, S. J. (2000). *Volunteering to help the environment.* New York: Scholastic Library.

Newell, P. (2000). *Volunteering to help seniors.* New York: Scholastic Library.

Perry, S. K. (2000). *Catch the spirit: Teen volunteers tell how they made a difference.* New York: Scholastic Library.

Rusin, J. B. (1999). *Volunteers wanted: A practical guide for getting and keeping volunteers.* Mobile, AL: Magnolia Mansions Press.

Ryan, B. (1998). *Community service for teens: Helping the ill, the poor, and the elderly.* Chicago: Ferguson.

Schwartz, L. (1994). *How can you help?: Creative volunteer projects for kids who care.* Huntington Beach, CA: Creative Teaching Press.

Waldman, J. (2000). *Teens with the courage to give: Young people who triumphed over tragedy and volunteered to make a difference.* York Beach, ME: Red Wheel/Weiser.

Wandberg, R. (2001). *Volunteering: Giving back.* Mankato, MN: Capstone Press.

Weeldryer, L. (2001). *Everything you need to know about volunteering.* New York: Rosen.

> **"***I believe that any definition
> of a successful life in America
> must include service to others ...
> serving others does mean rolling up your sleeves
> and getting involved in your community.
> It means getting off the sidelines—
> being a doer and not a critic.
> It means contributing to a cause larger than yourself.***"**
> —George P. Bush

Organizations

America's Promise
909 N. Washington St., Ste. 400
Alexandria, VA 22314-1556
Phone: (703) 684-4500; Fax: (703) 535-3900
E-mail: commit@americaspromise.org
http://www.americaspromise.org
Mobilizes people from every sector of American life to build the character and competence of our nation's youth by fulfilling five promises for young people.

Corporation for National and Community Service
1201 New York Ave., NW
Washington, DC 20525
Phone: (202) 606-5000

http://www.nationalservice.org
Helps Americans of all ages and backgrounds engage in service.

Kids Korp, USA
265 Santa Helena, Ste. 110-A
Solana Beach, CA 92075
Phone: (858) 259-3602; Fax: (858) 259-3603
E-mail: info@kidskorps.org
http://www.kidskorps.org
Engages young people (ages 5–18) in charitable activities and community-based service.

National 4-H Council
7100 Connecticut Ave.
Chevy Chase, MD 20815
Phone: (301) 961-2973
E-mail: info@fourhcouncil.edu
http://www.fourhcouncil.edu
Assists youth in developing knowledge, skills, and attitudes that will enable them to become productive and contributing members of society.

National Service Learning Clearinghouse
ETR Associates
4 Carbonero Way
Scotts Valley, CA 95066
Phone: (866) 245-7378; Fax: (831) 430-9471
E-mail: nslc@servicelearning.org
http://www.servicelearning.org
Supports the service-learning community in higher education, kindergarten through grade 12, community-based initiatives, and tribal programs, as well as all others interested in strengthening schools and communities using service-learning techniques and methodologies.

The Points of Light Foundation
and the Volunteer Center National Network
1400 I St., NW, Ste. 800
Washington, DC 20005
Phone: (800) 750-7653; Fax: (202) 729-8100
E-mail: info@pointsoflight.org
http://www.pointsoflight.org
Works to involve more people in effective volunteering.

Youth Service America
1101 15th St., Ste. 200
Washington, DC 20005
Phone: (202) 296-2992; Fax: (202) 296-4030
E-mail: info@ysa.org
http://www.ysa.org
A resource center of organizations committed to increasing the quantity and quality of opportunities for young Americans to serve locally, nationally, or globally.

Youth Volunteer Corps of America
4600 West 51st St., Ste. 300
Overland Park, KS 66205
Phone: (913) 432-9822; Fax: (913) 432-3313
E-mail: mrichmond@yvca.org
http://www.yvca.org
National network that creates volunteer opportunities to enrich America's youth, address community needs, and develop a lifetime commitment to service.

Part 4: Philanthropy

"It is wonderful to aspire and to achieve.
But success rings hollow
unless you remember your humanity along the way."
—Deborah Roberts

What is philanthropy?

Philanthropy is a love of humankind shown by practical kindness and helpfulness to humanity. A philanthropist is a person who loves humankind and works for its welfare, especially by giving donations of money to worthy causes. Raising or giving money to charitable causes helps children, youth, and adults who are needy in some way. They may need books, clothing, food, housing, and so forth. If everyone gives a little bit, great things will be accomplished.

How do I become a philanthropist?

When you are thinking about raising or giving money, look for a cause that involves your interests and talents. If you have an interest in reading, perhaps you would like to give money to a school reading program, donate books to the Boys and Girls Club, or develop a fundraising event to secure funds for your school or public library.

One of the first steps is to investigate the organization to which the funds will be directed. Most charities are honest and accountable to their donors. The American Institute of

Philanthropy (http://www.charitywatch.org) offers some guidelines for making donations of money.

Additional Cautions and Tips

Always know the charity. Never give to an organization that you know nothing about. Secure written information and a copy of the annual report. You should find a listing of board members, a mission statement, and information on audited financial statements. If these types of information are not available, you may wish to select another charity.

Always find out where your dollars go. You should determine how much of your donation goes to administrative services and what percent is directed to program services. The American Institute of Philanthropy's *Charitable Rating Guide* suggests that 60% or more should go to program services.

Do not respond to pressure. If you are not familiar with a charity/organization, do not give on the spot, but request additional information as to the purpose or nature of the group. You have the right to say no. Do not be engaged by emotional appeals. The "sob" story and the hard luck appeals are two common ways to try to get money. Again, ask questions about the nature of the organization and how the money is used.

Keep records of your donations. Do not give cash. Give a gift by check or money order to have an accurate record of your donation. With a donation of $250 or more the Internal Revenue Service (IRS) requires that you obtain a receipt from the charity.

The charity's name may be misleading. Some questionable charitable groups use impressive names to capture donors. Ask for information in writing and check out the organization. There are several groups to turn to for information. One is the American Institute on Philanthropy and another is your state charity registration.

One way to establish the authenticity of the organization is to determine if the charity is registered by local/state and federal authorities. Currently, 36 states require charities to register annually. A word of caution. A registered charity is not a stamp of approval.

Be careful of charities offering gifts by direct mail such as greeting cards, address stickers, key rings, and other items. You are not under any obligation to make a contribution. It is against the law for a charity to demand payment for any unordered gifts. The enclosed gifts may mean more fundraising costs for the organization.

Give generously according to your ability. When you have determined the charity is worthwhile, give at a rate with which you are comfortable. Wise giving is effective giving.

"Giving helps the giver
as much as those to whom the gift goes.
It broadens the vision and enlarges life.
It cultivates love, sympathy, and kindness.
It develops nobility of character
and generosity of conduct."

—Unknown

Web Sites

American Institute of Philanthropy (AIP)
http://www.charitywatch.org
Offers data on charities to help donors make informed decisions.

Women in Philanthropy
http://www.women-philanthropy.umich.edu/donors
Offers a large list of known female philanthropists.

Charity America
http://www.charityamerica.com
An online "village" that unites donors, volunteers, businesses, and qualified charities from across the nation.

The Chronicle of Philanthropy:
The Newspaper of the Nonprofit
http://www.philanthropy.com
News source for people involved in philanthropy.

Fundraisinginfo.com: Fundraising's Homepage
http://www.fundraisinginfo.com
Fundraising consultant company.

Give.org: Wise Giving Alliance
http://www.give.org
A profile of charities.

Guidestar: The National Database of Organizations
http://www.guidestar.org
Database of nonprofit organizations.

National Center for Charitable Statistics
http://www.nccs.urban.org

Provides financial and descriptive data on nonprofit organizations.

National Committee for Responsive Philanthropy
http://www.ncrp.org
Membership organization formed to help make organized philanthropy more responsive.

Philanthropy.org
http://www.philanthropy.org
Offers philanthropic trends information.

**Philanthropy Journal: Your Online
Source for Nonprofit News**
http://www.philanthropyjournal.org
Informative site that offers information to help understand, support, and work in the philanthropic world.

Philanthropy News Digest
http://www.fdncenter.org/pnd
Philanthropy news.

PNN Online
http://www.pnnonline.org
Nonprofit news and information resource.

Women and Philanthropy
http://www.womenphil.org
Advocates within the field of philanthropy for the full engagement of women and girls in society.

Women's Philanthropy Institute
http://www.women-philanthropy.org
Educates and encourages women in philanthropy.

"*Do what you can, with what you have, wherever you are.*"
—Theodore Roosevelt

Books

Bremner, R. H., & Boor, D. J. (1990). *American philanthropy.* Chicago: University of Chicago Press.

Bundles, A. (2001). *On her own ground: The life and times of Madame C. J. Walker.* New York: Atria Books.

Dowie, M. (2001). *American foundations: An investigative history.* Cambridge, MA: MIT Press.

Gary, T., & Kohner, M. (1998). *Inspired philanthropy: Creating a giving plan, a workbook.* New York: Wiley.

Gordon, B. (1998). *Bazaars and fair ladies: The history of the American fundraising fair.* Knoxville: University of Tennessee Press.

January, B. (1998). *De Witt and Lila Wallace: Charity for all.* New York: Scholastic Library.

Klein, K. (2000). *Fundraising for social change* (4th ed.). New York: Wiley.

Levchuck, C. M. (1999). *Learning about charity from the life of Princess Diana.* New York: Rosen.

McCarthy, K. D. (Ed.). (1990). *Lady bountiful revisited: Women, philanthropy, and power.* New Brunswick, NJ: Rutgers University Press.

McCarthy, K. D. (Ed.). (2001). *Women, philanthropy, and civil society.* Bloomington: Indiana University Press.

Meltzer, M. (1994). *Who cares? Millions do ...: A book about altruism.* New York: Walker.

Nielsen, W. A. (1999). *Golden donors: A new anatomy of the great foundations.* Pipcataway, NJ: Transaction.

O'Connell, H. (1993). *Dedicated lives: Women organizing for a fairer world.* Oxford, England: Oxfam.

Panas, J. (1998). *Mega gifts.* Chicago: Precept Press.

Prince, R. A., & File, K. M. (2001). *The seven faces of philanthropy: A new approach to cultivating major donors.* New York: Wiley.

Poppendieck, J. (1999). *Sweet charity: Emergency food and the end of entitlement.* New York: Penguin Putnam.

Rafferty, R. J. (1999). *Don't just give it away: How to make the most of your charitable giving.* Madison, WI: Chandler House.

Salzman, J., & Salzman, J. (1998). *Making the news: A guide for nonprofits and activists.* Boulder, CO: Westview Press.

Shaw, S. C. (with Taylor, M.). (1995). *Reinventing fundraising: Realizing the potential of women's philanthropy.* San Francisco: Jossey-Bass.

Shore, B. H., & Shore, W. H. (2001). *The cathedral within: Transforming your life by giving something back.* New York: Random House.

Sturtevant, W. T. (1997). *The artful journey: Cultivating and soliciting the major gift.* Chicago: Bonus Books.

Traub, C. G. (1997). *Philanthropists and their legacies.* Minneapolis, MN: Oliver Press.

❝*No act of kindness, no matter how small, is ever wasted.***❞**
—Aesop

Organizations

American Association of Fundraising Counsel
10293 N. Meridian St., Ste. 175
Indianapolis, IN 46290
Phone: (317) 816-1613; Fax: (317) 816-1633
E-mail: info@aafrc.org
http://www.aafrc.org
A professional organization dedicated to advancing philanthropy and assuring the highest ethical standards and professional practices.

American Institute of Philanthropy
3450 Lake Shore Dr.
P.O. Box 578460
Chicago, IL 60657
Phone: (773) 529-2300; Fax: (773) 529-0024
E-mail: aip@charitywatch.org
http://www.charitywatch.org
Produces the quarterly Charity Rating Guide, *including the* Charity Watchdog Report, *which informs donors on how approximately 400 national charities spend their money and*

keeps donors informed on current issues related to charitable giving. Also, Tips for Giving Wisely *is available with information on getting the most for your donated dollar and other valuable information.*

America's Charities
14150 Newbrook Dr.
Ste. 110
Chantilly, VA 20151
Phone: (800) 458-9505; Fax: (703) 222-3867
http://www.charities.org
A coalition of the nation's best-known and most-loved charitable organizations.

The National Center for Family Philanthropy
1818 N St., NW, Ste. 300
Washington, DC 20036
Phone: (202) 293-3424; Fax: (202) 293-3395
E-mail: ncfp@ncfp.org
http://www.ncfp.org
Encourages families and individuals to create and sustain their philanthropic missions.

The One Percent Club
2516 Chicago Ave.
Minneapolis, MN 55404
Phone: (612) 813-3240; Fax: (612) 874-6444
E-mail: info@onepercentclub.org
http://www.onepercentclub.org
An association of people of means dedicated to giving 1% or more of their net worth, or 5% of their income, whichever is greater, annually, to the charity of their choice.

Part 5: Girls' Stories

"One person can make a difference and every person should try."

—John F. Kennedy

Extraordinary accomplishments have been demonstrated by girls and young women in donating money, volunteering, and taking positive actions. You will be truly inspired as you read these amazing stories. Each contains details about setting goals and accomplishing them. The determination and planning of each one is remarkable.

Reflect on the advice each girl gives. Their words of wisdom should be inspiring as you go forward and enhance your abilities in becoming an empowered girl.

Leah Bitounis
Westlake, OH

Leah was born Glykeria C. Bitounis on June 21, 1985, to Gus and Catherine Bitounis. She lives in Westlake, OH, with her parents and her younger brother, Taki. After attending public school, Leah switched schools and began attending Hathaway Brown School in fourth grade, where she first discovered her love of service. Outside of her philanthropic and service endeavors, Leah's passions include photography, literature, history, writing, world affairs, and travel. She also participates in a scientific research project at the Hematology/Oncology Department at Case Western Reserve University. Her tenacity, drive, and dedication are what allow her to whole-heartedly and successfully pursue her goals.

Service Learning

One of the greatest accomplishments over the past 5 years has been the fact that I have been able to consistently find and take advantage of as many service opportunities as possible. It is my continuous participation in various service activities in different capacities that has allowed me to develop into a truly dedicated and knowledgeable contributor to the community. My enthusiasm for service began when I joined the Service Learning Club during my seventh-grade year at Hathaway Brown School for girls. I gradually took on responsibilities such as organizing and planning service activities. As an eighth grader, I took on my first official leadership position in a service organization by becoming the copresident of the club. During the same year, I became one of eight students who began to plan and develop a student-run foundation. The G.R.O.W. (Girls Reaching Others Worldwide) Foundation, as it was later named, did not take its final form until a year after I went on to high school.

I continued to pursue my interests in service through the opportunities that were available to me at my high school. I am currently the covice-president of the Service Learning Club in my school, the Order of Willing Service, which is also a position that transfers into a copresidency next year when I become a senior. I have participated in an after-school tutoring program at Harvey Rice Elementary School, a local, underfunded public school. Working with first through fourth graders on their reading skills and homework has been an amazing opportunity. The fact that I have been lucky enough to work with many of the same students for the past 2 years and will hopefully continue working with them over the next 2 years, as well, has only made this experience more rewarding. The chance to get to know and spend time with amazing kids has been one of my most rewarding experiences. Another project I have been lucky enough to be a part of is the Storks Nest Program. This program is operated through Huron Hospital and is run by the head of women's health for the area's local hospitals. It is a program where at-risk and expectant mothers attend a seminar once a month and are then able to amass points that can be used to purchase clothes, toys, and other items for their children. Having participated in this program for nearly a year now, I have been able to get to know the women and their babies. I have also been able to watch the program grow from serving only a few mothers to the point where a new location had to be found in order to accommodate the growing number of participants.

I have explored service opportunities outside of my school within the broader Cleveland community. I was able to do this primarily because of experiences I amassed through my service activities at Hathaway Brown. The organizations with which I have been most closely involved are the Mandel Center at Case Western Reserve University and Youth Philanthropy and Service (YPS), which is a division within the Mandel Center. The Mandel Center and YPS are one of the primary resources for nonprofit organizations, teachers, and youths in the Cleveland area that are involved with developing service learning and community service activities. I began my relationship with these organizations as a freshman when I applied and was accepted as a student member of a planning committee for YPS's annual service learning workshop/conference. I was fortunate enough to be offered one of only two student positions on the Mandel Center's advisory committee, which is essentially the Center's board. This experience has been particularly rewarding because of the recognition I have been given from the adults and professionals with whom I work on the committee. They have encouraged me to voice my opinions and have listened and respected them.

Being able to meet and get to know all of the people who run and participate in these various programs has been the most fascinating part of my service experiences. The things that I have learned are what I will always carry with me as I continue to incorporate service experiences into my life.

Katharine Grier Chambers
Oradell, NJ

Katharine Grier Chambers was born February 21, 1987. Katie lives with her parents, Susan and Peter, and their three dogs in Oradell, NJ, a suburb of Manhattan. Katie attends River Dell Regional High School. She has a deep appreciation of music and is a member of the River Dell Select Choir and plays the alto saxophone in the Wind Ensemble and Jazz Band. Katie created the River Dell Music Makers, a group comprised of students who raise money for the music department through multiple refreshment sales throughout the school year. She also plays the piano, took jazz dance lessons for 11 years, and recently earned her Cadette Girl Scout Silver Award and is now working toward her Gold Award. Her interests include musical theater and baseball (she is a huge Yankees fan). Katie's empathy and compassion help her when working with others, and her energy and focus enable her to do her best at any community service project in which she is involved.

Giving Back to the Village

Community service is something in which I believe everyone should take part. Like the old saying goes, "It takes a village to raise a child." Once that child has been raised, it is his or her responsibility to thank the *village* for everything it has done. My parents taught me the importance of giving back to the community, and I get great satisfaction from helping others.

My journey in community service starts like many others. It was a dark and stormy night—the first night of the blizzard of 1996. It was around 11 o'clock and my parents were still outside shoveling the snow to clear our driveway, and I was helping them as much as any 8-year-old could. As I watched the snow piling up in my elderly neighbor's driveway, I realized that she had no one to shovel it for her and, if she got into trouble, she would not be able to get out of her house. So, I went over and shoveled the driveway and walkway myself. I felt relieved in knowing that Mrs. Henry was safe in her house, and I felt good about myself because I had helped her. From that point on I decided to help my community in any way I could.

One of the best organizations where you can help others is the Girl Scouts. As Brownies in second and third grade, our activities focused mostly on crafts. These crafts, for example, were stuffed animals given to needy children or Christmas ornaments given as a "thank you" to families who donated clothing to the homeless during the holidays. After researching the negative effects of smoking on your health, we made anti-smoking posters and hung them throughout the halls of Oradell Public School. Every December our troop visited Sunbridge Nursing Home to sing Christmas carols with the patients.

As Junior Girl Scouts in fourth through sixth grade, we worked with younger troops to help them earn badges and learn about different careers and how to deal with tough issues like peer pressure. Girl Scouts gives you the opportunity to have fun as a group and help your community at the same time.

As Cadettes in seventh through ninth grade, most of our activities focused on earning our Silver Award, the highest level of achievement at that level for Girl Scouts. Our first 2 years as Cadettes were spent completing the prerequisites for the award. We had to earn three badges, all of which require some form of community service to complete. For example, to earn the "Rolling Along" badge, our troop held a bike rally and taught younger children about bike safety. To earn the Cadette Girl Scout Challenge, the next requirement, I helped run craft booths at the Oradell Winterfest and made posters for Girl Scout Recruitment Night. Finally, we each had to earn the Cadette Girl Scout Leadership Award, which requires each scout to lead community service activities for a total of 25 hours. I completed this by helping a younger troop tour the Statue of Liberty and Ellis Island, cooking and serving dinner to the homeless, and volunteering at the Oradell Public Library during the summer.

Our last year as Cadettes, we actually designed and carried out our Silver Award Project, which is a personal action plan for helping others that must include community service. The planning and execution of the project have to take a minimum of 30 hours, with 7 to 10 hours devoted to the actual implementation of the project. We brainstormed several project ideas and decided to share our love for our country, which seemed especially important after September 11. We named our project Operation American Spirit and our mission was to share a practical, hands-on view of patriotism with other Oradell Girl Scouts.

Our troop developed a presentation to be given to the younger scouts that would explore the many aspects of patriotism and included fun games and crafts. We each researched and prepared the parts that appealed to us most,

and, when the Girl Scout Council came out with new patriotism badges, we tailored our presentation so that the girls
could earn a badge, as well. It was my responsibility to
research patriotic music, the history of the flag, and how to
care for it. Our presentation also included a flag ceremony,
flag folding, American landmarks, and the definition of
patriotism. We each had to be familiar with one another's
topics in case we had to cover for each other.

We visited 16 different troops over the course of 3
months, a total of 177 scouts. Another troop member and I
were also invited to present to 40 second graders at Oradell
Public School on Flag Day. The Oradell post of the
American Legion signed our award papers after we gave
them a summary of our project. We received our Silver
Award.

I faced many difficult obstacles while working toward
my Silver Award. The biggest problem was getting the troop
leaders to respond to my phone calls. They would express
their interest in our project and ask us to come to their
meetings, but many did not call me back for scheduling. I
found myself spending hours at the kitchen table making
phone calls and praying they would call me back to confirm.
It took a lot of self-control and determination, but I was able
to keep everything in order. Another problem I faced was
how to keep a room full of 30 screaming 8-year-olds in line!
I used my quick sense of humor and love and understanding of children to keep everyone entertained and focused at
the same time.

The biggest obstacle I faced while earning the Silver
Award (and perhaps the biggest of my entire life) was my
grandfather's passing. He was very important and a great
source of inspiration to me. After watching his suffering
with emphysema, I was emotionally drained. I found it very
difficult to concentrate on my goals for Girl Scouts, but the
loving support from my family and friends and my own

stubbornness and determination (qualities my grandfather had passed down to me) kept me going.

Community service is a vital part of my life. I have been able to help others, boost my self-esteem, gain additional self-confidence, learn to respect all people, and make lifelong friends. I plan to continue giving back to the "village that raised me" for the rest of my life.

Victoria Copland
Clinton, MS

Victoria Copland is from Clinton, MS. She was born in Jackson, MS, on March 20, 1988. When she was a baby, she moved with her family to Alaska, where they stayed about 18 months. Victoria and her father moved to Clinton, which has been their home since. She attends Central Hinds Academy, where she is the treasurer of the Art Club. She also plays on the Lady Cougar's fastpitch softball team. She likes to write poetry and songs, spend time with her friends, talk on the phone, and listen to pop, rock, country, and rap music.

Pens to Bosnia

When I was in seventh grade, my friend Maggie Blair and I had an idea to help students in Bosnia. Maggie's father is a member of the U.S. Armed Forces, and he had been stationed in Bosnia. He told Maggie what life was like in Bosnia, and she invited him to speak to our class at school. We were all touched by the descriptions of the students just like us attending school in buildings that were war-torn. The classes in Bosnia are large, their pencils are taped together, and sometimes several students even have to share one pencil.

Coincidentally, my aunt was on a trip to Bosnia when Maggie's dad talked to us. When my aunt returned, she showed me photographs of the bullet holes in schools, buildings with no outside walls, dark classrooms, and kids who looked pretty much like the ones in my own school. I thought about what it would be like to go to school every day in a place like that and what it would be like to have to share a broken pencil with a whole table of other students.

Maggie and I thought we should do something to help these children. I suggested that we collect school supplies to send to Bosnia. Maggie talked to our principal, Mr. Noonan, who approved our idea. Our team of 120 students, called the Blazers, collected paper, pens, pencils, and other school supplies. I visited the manager of the local Office Depot, who was interested in helping, but needed to call my school before he donated. After he had checked with the school, the Office Depot donated 250 pens.

Maggie's dad helped us ship five boxes of supplies that we had collected. Two of those boxes were filled with the pens from Office Depot. It made me feel really good to know that these supplies would help a student in need.

At the end of the school year, Maggie received an award for getting so many people to participate. Maggie asked to use the microphone to say something to the audience. She thanked the teachers for the award, but I was really surprised when she said, "I wouldn't have had the idea unless Victoria Copland had suggested it." My teachers made me stand up on my seat and the whole school applauded.

I think everyone at our school was generous—not just Maggie and I—but all of us. I hope we do a similar project again and strive for other things: notebooks, small calculators, educational posters, batteries, and calendars. We could also send money so they could get P. E. uniforms, new desks, lights, air conditioners, and heaters. I'm sure they would appreciate everything we provide them.

I feel really good knowing I helped people just by getting them pens so they could write without having to pass it back and forth. I like to write. I write for myself, not just for schoolwork, and I would loathe having to pass a pen back and forth. How would you like to have to share a pen with other people? How would you do your homework? I think it would be really difficult. Learning about the students in Bosnia and helping them made me appreciate being an American. As an American, I never have to worry about whether there will be pens, pencils, and paper on which to write.

Maddy Coquillette
Cleveland Hts., OH

Maddy Coquillette attends Hathaway Brown School in Shaker Heights, OH. She was born October 13, 1987. She lives in Cleveland Heights with her mom and dad, older brother, younger sister, and a yellow Labrador retriever. She is captain of her school's junior varsity tennis team and plays on the basketball team. As an honor student who enjoys math and science, she is excited about beginning an independent science research project this year. She plays piano and guitar and enjoys travel, reading, and spending time with her friends. Her work with special-needs children and adults meshes perfectly with her positive, outgoing, and empathetic personality.

Special-Needs Children and Adults

Over the past 2 years I have reached out and touched the lives of more than 100 special-needs children and adults. This past summer I dedicated myself to working with seven unique children, all of whom had visual impairments, as well as other disabilities. My work took place in an early intervention program for visually impaired children between the ages of 3 and 5 years. I met with these seven young children, three boys and four girls, each with varying levels of vision impairment and other disabilities, each day as they attended Bright Futures Preschool at the Cleveland Sight Center. Along with several other adults, I worked to meet the needs of these special children in such areas as language, self-help, fine and gross motor abilities, prereading skills, pre-Braille, mobility, the use of their residual vision, and social skills. The work I did with these children resulted in an extraordinary experience, greatly influencing both their lives and mine.

Out of all of the children attending the Bright Futures Preschool, a young boy touched me the most. Although the preschool specializes in vision impairments, many of the children have other disabilities, as well, such as this child. In addition to his severe visual disability, he faced developmental delays. At the age of 3, he had just learned to walk, eat solid foods, and speak and had just begun many of the activities of a normal toddler. It was amazing to me how much I was able to teach him in only 2 months, and I watched him flourish as he began to understand the world around him. I could see that he had the energy and excitement equal to, if not more than, any 3-year-old, and with my help he was able to do so many new things and grow. Throughout the summer as I worked with him and the other children, I felt I had made a clear, positive difference in each of their lives.

Although these children are capable of many of the

behaviors of an average 3-year old, there are many differences. All of the children in this program were noticeably smaller than other children their age, and many of them were just beginning to develop abilities that most children acquire long before 3 years of age. Unlike an average preschooler, who uses words and sentences frequently to express his or her thoughts and ideas, for these children it was a great accomplishment to use even three or four words together in any form. This was one area that I worked on extensively throughout the summer with each child. Seemingly small accomplishments for most children are huge steps to these children. Putting a simple three-piece puzzle together, blowing bubbles, recognizing colors, learning the alphabet, counting, and singing along to typical nursery songs all seem like normal activities for a young child, but were extremely challenging for these children.

When I look back on my experience, I realize how special each of the preschoolers I worked with that summer really is, and being able to make such an impact in their lives has given me a great feeling of accomplishment. They struggle with so many things each day that most of us have never faced, and yet they are so full of life, ready to try anything.

Another quality I found in many of these children was their ability to concentrate intently on one project, usually a very small action that most would never think of as an activity at all. Once, while I was supervising several children and a young boy at the sensory table, we put dry noodles of various shapes and forms on the table. A few of the children were able to use their refined sensory skills to take the noodles and string them on a shoestring, but the boy, because his motor control was severely limited, was not able to perform this activity. Instead, I gave him a small plastic cup and a spoon and I guided his hands to show him how to use the spoon to pick up noodles and place them in the cup. After several seconds, he took the spoon on his own, and I could see the intense look on his face as he very carefully scooped up one or two noodles and guided the spoon into the cup. Over and over again he repeated this until the cup was full of noodles. Then he searched with his hands and found another cup on the table and very cautiously poured all of the contents from one cup to the other, over and over again, back and forth, from his right to left hand. As I watched this tiny boy perform this task—not a simple task for him by any means—I asked him what he was doing with the noodles. He responded in a very small, yet serious voice, "I pour them." For him, this was wonderful. He not only was able to control his motor skills necessary to complete this task, but he also was able to put words together to tell me what he was doing, both of which are extremely hard for him.

I have a great number of stories to tell about my interactions with special-needs children and adults. During the past 2 years, I have provided music therapy for memory-impaired residents at the McGregor Retirement Community; served as a counselor at Champ Camp, a summer program for multiply disabled children ages 4 to 8 years; helped weekly at the Cleveland Sight Center in a program for visually impaired preteens and teenagers; tutored in special education classes in a municipal school for disabled children; and worked as a teacher's assistant in a first-grade classroom. Although I am mainly dedicated to working with children, I have worked with both children and adults with epilepsy, cerebral palsy, glaucoma, spina bifida, vision impairments, motor control restrictions, autism, Alzheimer's disease, and many other disabilities. I have worked with children in wheelchairs, with feeding tubes, on respirators, and using walkers; children who have suffered brain strokes; and those with extreme speech and motor disabilities, burn injuries, and other multiple disabilities.

Through these experiences, I have encountered many situations with which most teenagers would never deal and that many people would find very difficult. When around those with such severe disabilities, most people are intimidated and uncomfortable, and it makes me extremely proud to be able to say that I have never felt this way. I have learned that each has a unique collection of needs, and I have extended myself to each individual in order to understand how to help them best.

My interactions with special-needs children have benefited me in many ways. I have been a positive influence in the lives of all of the children with whom I have worked, and each of them has undoubtedly changed my life, too. My experiences have taught me a great deal about myself, how to relate to others, and has shown me how my outgoing nature can really help light up the world of those around me. After each experience, I find myself having much more confidence in my abilities. When I enter a new situation or opportunity, I feel I can do more and more each time.

The biggest struggle for me has been my age. In every program in which I have participated, I have been the youngest volunteer. One of the major obstacles I face is trying to find programs that will accept a volunteer my age. Many program directors are skeptical that a teenager is capable of doing the type of work in which I have been involved. In some cases, even after being accepted as a volunteer, I have found that I had to work extra hard to overcome the initial cautiousness of a few staff members. Convincing others of my seriousness is not the only challenge I have faced, but it is the only one I find most frustrating. Hopefully, now that I have more experience and many people who can provide positive references regarding my abilities, it will be easier.

Other challenges I have encountered have included learning to relate to many different kinds of people and dealing with the particular characteristics of young children. In my volunteering, I have almost always worked with individuals who are different from me in terms of age, maturity level, physical and mental ability, and economic and cultural background. Each group requires me to provide a different type of support, and to do that, I must adjust myself to each unique situation and the special needs of the particular group. I do not focus on the differences between us, but I try to understand how best to communicate with each person.

Working with any group of children can be a challenge because they are unpredictable and can behave in ways that sometimes seem unreasonable. It is impossible to always be prepared, and it can be a real test of skill to adapt to each circumstance as it arises. I have especially noticed the physical and mental differences that occur even between two children in the same program. After spending some time with each child, I can understand what types of language and actions work best, and I incorporate them into the way I approach my role. One of the concepts I struggled with this past summer was judging when to allow a child to experience the consequences of his or her actions in order to learn and when to be slightly more lenient. If I am unsure of a child's capabilities or how he or she might react to a different approach, I engage myself with that child and begin to teach myself about how he or she functions. This approach has shown me just how many different methods can be used to enhance the way a particular child learns and grows. The work I do greatly influences each child's progress, and I know that in each situation there are many aspects that must be considered.

Many people have asked me how I became involved with this type of work, as I clearly enjoy it to an unusual degree for a teen. As a young girl, I was interested in volunteer work, and the summer before eighth grade, I decided to join a program in which a family friend had been involved, a summer camp for multiply disabled children under the age of 8. It took a great deal of effort to become a counselor in this program, but after being introduced to these children, it became clear to me that I loved working with them. I was particularly interested in helping and interacting with those with special needs. As the youngest counselor, I seemed to have talent and passion for working with these children. After the summer session, I felt compelled to find another similar placement, which brought me to the Cleveland Sight Center.

I encourage all others, teens and adults, to become engaged in volunteer work because it brings a feeling of self-fulfillment and is a positive aspect of my life that I could not replace with anything. I cannot imagine who I would be if I had not gotten involved in these activities. I find courage within myself, and I find that it is an outgoing manner that works best for me when I work with these children. I have a strong attitude of "just do it." As it is very easy to become overwhelmed by the responsibilities, worry about the decisions you must make, and become nervous or unsure regarding how to deal with each child's unique personality and disabilities, I find the best thing to do is just go for it.

Debbie Dietrich
Charles City, IA

Deborah Emily Dietrich was born on December 19, 1985, in Mason City, IA. She currently lives in Charles City, IA. She is the only child of Drs. Bruce and Deborah Dietrich, both of whom are practicing veterinarians. Debbie will complete her secondary education as a member of the graduating class of 2004 at Charles City High School. Her favorite subjects include science, biology, math, and art. She is a member of the student council, varsity girls' basketball, and junior varsity girls' golf, and she plays the piccolo in the Charles City High School marching band and the flute in the symphonic band. She has received first-place awards in science fairs, speech contests, and essay writing contests, and she has made numerous honor band appearances. In 2000, she received the Girl Scout Silver Award, and in 2003 she received the highest recognition that the Girl Scouts offers, the Gold Award.

Repainting the Suspension Bridge

I have been a member of Girl Scouts for 10 years. I wanted to achieve the highest award that the Girl Scouts offers—the Gold Award. Less than 1% of the 2.5 million registered Girl Scouts receive this lifetime award, which symbolizes outstanding accomplishments in the areas of leadership, community service, career planning, and personal development. The Girl Scout Gold Award consists of five segments: earning four interest patches, the Career Exploration Pin, the Senior Girl Scout Leadership Award, the Senior Girl Scout Challenge, and implementing a Girl Scout Gold Award Project. The project should benefit the community with 50 hours of work, and all expenses incurred in the project are the responsibility of the scout and must be completely raised by her.

For my community service portion of the Gold Award, I chose to repaint the suspension bridge in my hometown of Charles City, IA. The bridge was placed on the National Historic Register on October 30, 1989. The bridge was constructed in 1906 by the Hart Parr Company, manufacturer of the first tractor, and donated to the city of Charles City. It is 467 feet long and 4 feet wide, and is suspended by two 45-foot-tall steel towers encased in concrete piers. The support system consists of 14 x-shaped vertical steel supports ranging in height from 6 to 32 feet and 78 vertical support rods varying in size from 3 to 40 feet tall. The commercial estimate to repaint the suspension bridge was $25,000. At the completion of my project, more than 500 hours of labor had been donated by me, my family, and friends, and expenses were only $2,500. Through my fundraising efforts and the generosity of my community, I managed to raise $6,000. I hope to replace the 1,000 feet of fence on the bridge later this year with the remaining funds.

The suspension bridge in Charles City means a great deal to the community. In the summer, children use the bridge to get across town to the pool and the baseball fields without having to cross busy streets full of cars. Joggers, bikers, walkers, and people of all ages use the bridge to cross the scenic Cedar River and enjoy the peace and serenity of the area. The bridge is not only used for walking. It is outlined in lights and illuminated during special events in the town and for holidays. The bridge is the most beautiful when it is lit up during the Christmas season. It is a local landmark, and some think it gives the city its identity. Bus tours often make the bridge the highlight of their trip to Charles City.

The bridge has had an impact on my life. I live on the river downstream from the bridge and see it quite clearly from my house. It looked terrible and run down with all the paint peeling off. Many nights I have used the bridge to get to the other side of town, and I hated how bad it looked. It looks good now and will continue to serve the many generations of people in my town.

In preparation for my project, I had to interact with many people. Initially, I contacted the mayor of Charles City and gained the approval of the city for my project. I researched the history of the bridge to gain background information. I identified the scope of my project through inspection of all parts of the bridge and documented this information with photographs. I had numerous meetings with the suppliers of paint and equipment, the people who volunteered to work, and the appropriate city agencies. I prepared a cost estimate after meeting with suppliers, and I documented my meetings by keeping a daily journal. I also prepared a list of important names and phone numbers of people who were going to help me with my project, and I organized a labor force consisting of friends and family with a timetable for completing the project.

Communicating with small and large groups, organizing people and equipment, managing my time and the time of my volunteers, and working hard helped me accomplish my goal. Encouragement and help from my parents and the completion of each day's task boosted my courage to keep going and accomplish my goal. I have never started a project without completing it, and I knew if I put my mind to it, I would get through. I am glad I listened to my parents because they gave me the strength to become a better person and showed me how to succeed. The satisfaction of doing a good job and accomplishing something great had a positive influence on my life. After speaking in front of four large service groups, meeting with presidents of banks, and presenting my fundraising efforts to corporations and businesses alike, I overcame my fear of public speaking. Preparing my speech ahead of time, typing it up, practicing it at home, and staying calm before I presented helped conquer my fear of large groups. Appearing on television in front of the mayor and the city council to make my presentation about the bridge was my last hurdle. I know I made my parents very proud that night.

In spite of all the encouragement and help I received, the one thing that sticks in my mind is the fact that sometimes you can't rely on other people. Do not take on jobs that you cannot complete by yourself. I was not always able to get volunteers on the desired days to work even though they said they would help. On these days, I worked on the bridge alone. I learned that painting a bridge is not an easy task. I had the inner strength and desire to paint by myself those days, and this experience made me more confident in my abilities and more responsible for my actions. All of these positive and negative experiences have prepared me for the future.

I faced a few obstacles while undertaking my project. I had contacted our mayor in January requesting permission to paint the bridge. On June 14, he told me it had to be completed by July 4. My dad decided to take time off from his practice and work longer days with me to help get it done on time. The two main towers, extending 45 feet in the sky, became a very large obstacle for us to paint. My father and I obtained a safety harness and a paint sprayer so one of the volunteers could climb the tower and paint it safely. The understructure of the bridge posed the largest obstacle in finishing the painting project. Two pontoon boats, a bass boat, 15 volunteers, and the erection of a scaffold on the pontoon boat allowed us to finish the project.

I didn't think I would be able to raise the $2,500 necessary to pay for the paint and supplies, and I was worried about how to go about securing the money. I discussed the problem with the director of our Chamber of Commerce. The director gave me a list of potential donors and businesses that he thought would contribute money and a little pep talk on how to raise funds.

Without the help of many people, I would not have been able to complete my goal of painting the bridge. I would like to give recognition to those people. My parents, Drs. Bruce and Deb Dietrich, helped me the most. My dad guided me through the project and painted the higher, more difficult portions. He had experience in painting and using ladders and ropes. My mom kept me on task and encouraged me, giving me the necessary strength to keep going. The people and companies that provided equipment included: Young Construction, Hobert Electric, Charles City Street Department, Wubbens Electric, Sherwin-Williams, Charles City Parks Department, Streamline Painting, David Ayers, Ivan Reimer, and John Simon. The people who helped me paint and worked on the bridge included: Drs. Bruce and Deb Dietrich, Troy Mussman, Mallory McCauley, Erin Haffey, Samantha Sweet, Dave Sweet, Bob Woolm, Lindsey Nordaas, Julie Nordaas, Brianna Aspholm, John Simon, Ivan Reimer, Dr. David Shapiro, Leland Boyd, Delaine Freeseman, Susan Ayers, Cody Kiroff, Kurt Herbrechtsmeyer, Russ Berns, Brian Young, and Dick Young. I also have a long list of people and companies that donated money to the "Repainting of the Suspension Bridge Fund." All of these people helped make my project a success.

I think I would do this project again. The painting was difficult, but in the end, it all paid off. I enjoyed working with many people and learning new things. I liked being the person in charge of a large community project. I also enjoyed learning new skills from experienced adults in my community. The one thing I really liked is the fact that everyone in town knows who I am now and appreciates that I am a responsible, smart, determined, hard-working young woman. In Charles City, I now stand out in a crowd.

My mother is my female role model. She has had the biggest impact on my life. She is a doctor of veterinary medicine and works in research for an animal health company. She is very intelligent and is constantly working to improve herself at her job. My mom has shown me many things in my short life. She always encourages me to do my best, and her life accomplishments serve as an example. She always expects me to do my best and will do anything possible to help me do the best that I can. She has helped me so much that I don't know what I would do without her. I love her very much.

My advice for anyone undertaking a large community service project is to plan well in advance. Planning out the needed supplies, labor, and funding will be hard work, but any project you undertake will teach you so many valuable things for the future. Follow your dreams; you can do anything you put your mind to. Look at me—I painted a 467-foot suspension bridge!

Shireen Dogar
Madison, MS

Shireen Dogar was born in Macon, GA, on May 4, 1989. She has an inspiring older sister and a younger brother. In school, Shireen is active in the Beta Club, plays drums in the school band, and her favorite subject is science. The study of the human body fascinates her, and she hopes to become a surgeon some day. Shireen also enjoys painting, the outdoors, spending time with friends, playing Nintendo, and watching cartoons.

Building a Flowerbed

My charitable accomplishment was building the frame of a flowerbed for a first-grade class. I really wanted to pursue this charitable activity. I knew that it would surely delight the younger children if they could watch the plants grow into beautiful flowers. By adding flowers to the landscape, the school's appearance would also be brightened. I really wanted to spend some time outdoors and get close to nature, and I also desired to learn more about building things. However, the main reason I wanted to take part in this charitable activity was because it would be fun and bring me closer to my family since we would all be doing something together. I also knew this project would make me a better person.

Without any preparation before actually building the frame of the flowerbed, the task would have been very difficult. I went to bed earlier than usual the night before the big project to conserve energy and strength for the next day's work. I also did a few exercises to warm up my muscles and prevent tiring. I ate a good, healthy breakfast to provide the needed strength and packed all the necessary tools, including hammers and tape measures, as well as plenty of water and snacks to fuel our bodies during the long, hot day of building.

The building took place at Baker Elementary, a school with limited resources. The children attending the school come from disadvantaged backgrounds. Our idea would give the students a new, hands-on experience they would not forget. Once the flowerbed was complete, the first graders would be able to observe nature grow under certain conditions, and they could participate in hands-on outdoor projects to help them better understand the science of nature.

This project was very enjoyable and worthwhile. I was amused by the conversations we had while trying to dig out rusty, but reusable, nails from the slabs of wood. Even through hard work, our spirits remained high. Going through this experience taught me a lot of new lessons. Working hard and pacing myself was very important while building the flowerbed. I learned how to endure the heat of the day and the long hours of hard work, and now I know the endurance and training a builder goes through. My personal qualities have also been affected by participating in this volunteer activity. For example, I am joyous when I know that I'm helping someone else learn through nature, and I feel extremely proud of the accomplishment. I now know how it feels to be helpful. In addition, my craftsmanship has improved.

Many people assisted me in this project. My parents, older sister, and younger brother all helped. The teacher (for whom we were building the flowerbed) and her family also assisted. Pitching in helped get the job done quickly, and we still had time to fly kites and look back on the day. I could not have done it without everybody's help.

I will certainly volunteer in similar activities in the future. I feel contented and pleased with myself having accomplished this task. Helping other people is not a chore, but a privilege. It's not only fun, but provides a sensational feeling when you have done something good to benefit others. Participating and volunteering in community-related activities also allows others to see me as a helpful person.

My positive role model during the whole project would most certainly be my mom. She showed outstanding endurance throughout the whole day, and I was truly impressed by her unmistakable hard work. She always has a bright, cheerful smile on her face that reflects her positive mood. She works very hard, and she was the best of help to me during this project because she was always there, either giving me a glass of water or prying apart boards. She is very encouraging. I really appreciate the endless list of things my mom does for me. She pushes me to strive to my highest potential, and she is a hard-working woman. I really admire her good qualities and her advice and words of wisdom. I truly respect her.

My advice to others would be to get out and do something to benefit the community and the people around it. Volunteering has made me a better, hard-working person. Think about volunteering, and then think about the benefits. Volunteer for a great cause.

Amy Dykman
Brandon, MS

Amy Elizabeth Dykman was born on May 12, 1989, in Jackson, MS. Her parents are Stan and Jennifer Rasberry Dykman. Amy has one sibling, a brother, Craig Dykman. Amy has always been a people person with a smile for everyone, including total strangers. Her family moved to Brandon, MS, in 1993, where they still reside. She is an honor roll student whose favorite subjects include history and English. Amy also plays trombone, is an avid reader, and works as a library assistant during school. Amy is known for her smile, her kindness, her giving spirit, and her love for people. She remains humble in spite of her amazing accomplishments!

Bears Care and So Do We!

I was at school when we were told about the attacks on the World Trade Center and the Pentagon. I felt scared and confused and wished I was at home with my family, but our teachers assured us that we were safe at school. I am certain they were scared, too, but each did a good job of hiding it from us.

As the week passed, I felt scared, sad, and angry that someone could do something so horrible to all of those people. I especially felt sorry for the children who had lost a parent because I know how I would feel if something happened to my parents. I wanted to help, but I didn't know what a 12-year-old could do. Then a news show came on about the number of children whose parents had died and I knew what I needed to do.

I love my teddy bears. They have always given me comfort, and I decided that all of those children should have a teddy bear to hug. I sat down at the computer and printed up a flier to distribute. I called my project "Bears Care and So Do We." I talked to my mom and told her what I wanted to do, and she thought it was a great idea. So, that night, my dad took me to the grocery store and I used their copy machine to make copies of my fliers.

The next day I asked permission from my principal, Buddy Bailey, to distribute the fliers, and he thought it was a great idea. My mom called the grocery store where we shop and asked the manager, Wayne Estes, if we could use his lobby for a drop-off site for the bears I wanted to collect. When I got home from school that day, she told me that he had agreed to the request. She then asked me how many weeks I wanted to collect the bears and what my goal was. I told her that I would go to the grocery store every Saturday through October 27th, which was Make a Difference Day, and I wanted to collect at least 5,000 to 6,000 bears because that was how many children had lost a parent.

The next morning, before I left for school, I called the local radio station. I told the DJs, Rick Adams and Kim Allen, what I was going to do and that I wanted to let everyone know. Rick and Kim not only said they would spread the word, but would help me in any way they could. So, the radio station and all of their DJs reminded listeners every week to go by the designated grocery store in Brandon or by Brandon Middle School and drop off their bears.

My mom and I took our card table, two chairs, some balloons, a big box, and a poster I made telling people what I was doing and why, and we went to grocery store early that Saturday morning. We stayed at the store for 5 hours. Seventy-four bears were collected that first Saturday. Most of the people who brought the bears had heard me on the radio the day before. I was so excited! My mom and I had a really big surprise when a local television reporter came by and interviewed me. The station was WJTV, a CBS affiliate out of Jackson, MS. Somebody told us that we should let our local newspapers know so that even more people would bring bears, so we did and it worked!

I loved meeting the people and giving them hugs when they dropped off the bears. People told me that I was helping them feel better by doing something to help all of the children. I started to feel less afraid because my mind was on my bears. My mom told me that, even if I didn't reach my goal of 5,000 to 6,000 bears, I should be very proud of myself for what I was trying to do. She told me that she believed I would reach my goal because I could accomplish anything. There were days when we would go by the store to check to see if more bears had been donated and sometimes there weren't any, and I would feel disappointed. But, the next day, there might be 50 bears waiting for me! I never gave up and looked forward to going to the grocery store every Saturday (six in a row) to collect the bears. Also, the radio DJs, Kim Allen and Van Hazlitt, came to the grocery store and did a live broadcast to collect more bears. In 3 hours, 444 bears were collected!

I still needed a way to get all of my bears up to New York. KLLM Trucking Company called into the radio station and said they would see to it that my bears got delivered. My mom cried right there on the spot, and I was so happy. I was put in touch with a lady in New Jersey named Parry Aftab. Ms. Aftab then put me in touch with a girls' school in Demarest, NJ, called the Academy of the Holy Angels. The school requested that I ship the bears to them and they would put them in gift baskets to be passed out in New York to the victim's children. Everyone at this girls' school was happy to help because Christina Zisa, a student there, had lost her father at the World Trade Center on September 11.

On, Saturday, October 27th, Make a Difference Day, I collected more than 1,000 bears at the grocery store. By the time I was ready to ship the bears to New Jersey, 12,162 bears had been collected for the children of New York.

What did I learn? A lot. I learned that if a 12-year-old girl like me can accomplish a goal like this, anything can happen! Can one person make a difference? Yes. I am not a hero, just a girl who wanted to help. The real heroes are the victims and their families left behind, like Christina Zisa, who lost her father, Salvatore, and will not have him there to see her graduate from high school or share any of the special moments yet to come in her young life.

I am so blessed to still have my family. I met so many nice, charitable people who helped collect and ship the bears. The bears were passed out in New York on Friday, December 14, 2001. Even though I could not be there, I am so proud of what I did. I will probably never meet some of the people in New Jersey or New York who helped me, but I feel as if they are my friends anyway. I received Christmas cards from the girls at the Academy of the Holy Angels (16 in all), and I won a national Make A Difference Day award for my project. The Mayor of Brandon, Roe Grubbs, presented me with the first ever humanitarian award. I did not expect any awards, but was so proud to receive them.

Would I do my "Bears Care and So Do We" project again? Yes! But, I hope it is never for the same reason. I am already working on getting ready for this years' Make a Difference Day project, which will focus on illiteracy.

My female role models are my mother and Laura Bush, our First Lady. My mom always tries to do the right thing and has supported me in everything I have pursued. Mrs. Bush, whom I hope to meet one day, seems like such a nice woman who really cares about children. Also, I now have to add Parry Aftab in New Jersey, who founded Cyberangels and who helped me find a place to send my bears. She also works very hard to help children and keep them safe on the Internet.

My advice to other girls is that, if you feel strongly enough about what you want to achieve and are doing it for the right reasons, you are never too young. I was only 12. You will get back 10 times what you give. One person *can* make a difference. I did!

Karli Echterling
St. Joseph, MO

Karli Ross Echterling, daughter of Ron Echterling and Sharon and Mel Bradford, was born July 13, 1982. As a native of St. Joseph, MO, Karli has been actively involved in public and volunteer services and has contributed more than 1,300 hours to a variety of community organizations. In 2002, she was a recipient of the Gold Medal Congressional Award in Washington, DC. This award recognizes the initiative, achievement, and service of youth who challenge themselves and make a positive impact on their community. Karli's academic interests include biology, chemistry, and gerontology. Her research in gerontology has been recognized by four International Science and Engineering Fair Awards. Currently, Karli is a student at the University of Missouri and is the developer and director of the LIFE (Lasting Intergenerational Fellowship Experience) program. This program is designed to promote intergenerational relationships between youth and senior citizens. Upon completion of undergraduate studies, she will attend the University of Missouri School of Medicine as a Conley Scholar.

Pictures of Courage

"It's the camera lady!" These words became my title at Camp Quality, a camp for children with cancer. I had volunteered the previous summer as an activities assistant and was astounded by the lives these children were required to live. Their one-week vacation at camp provided a short period of normality for them. While many youth attend camps over the summer and must select which to attend, this camp is currently the only one in this area available to children with cancer. I was amazed by the pure joy they expressed for being at camp even though their daily routines included reminders of the disease they faced. I decided that there had to be something I could do to make the next year's camp even more memorable.

As I reflected on the camps I had attended, I realized I relived the memories every time I looked at my photographs. Through pictures, I could make the next camp a lasting memory for the children. With this as my mission, I decided to provide disposable cameras to all 100 campers, but faced the need for $600 to achieve this goal. Fortunately, as the recipient of a previous volunteer award, I was allowed to designate $250 to a charitable organization. Using that money and an additional $350 of donated funds, I was able to purchase the cameras. My excitement became contagious, and another volunteer offered to secure funds for film developing. Through our combined efforts, we were able to accomplish my mission.

Throughout the week of camp, I became acutely aware of how one small act of volunteering could affect the lives of so many people in a positive manner. The simple act of providing cameras opened an arena of opportunity for the children to select their own memories. The cameras became a common avenue of conversation and allowed the campers to become easily acquainted. As the new acquaintances quickly became old friends, I realized the cameras had served their purpose. Experiences had been shared, giggles and tears expressed, and a keepsake in their backpack provided a lasting reminder

My joy in providing for the children of Camp Quality led me to look for further ways to enhance their experiences at camp. In my previous visits to the campground, I recognized the rustic state of some of the cabins including broken doors, cracked steps, faded paint, and insufficient lighting. One cabin in particular, used by Camp Quality's Recreation Services, was in desperate need of repair. To further serve the needs of the program, I chose to renovate this staff cabin. The initial step included contacting the campground committee and requesting a meeting with the finance board. During this meeting with the representatives of the church who own the campground, I proposed my renovation for the staff cabin, cost estimates, and expected completion date. The campground finance board enthusiastically agreed to support this proposal and fund the estimated costs. With secured funds and an organized team of volunteers to assist, the renovation began.

As I began to square the windows and realign the front door, I realized the need to stop and rethink my plan. Initially, I had looked at the cabin as a "fix-it" project in need of some paint and tender loving care. Yet, as the project began to take a new form, I came to recognize the importance of a strong foundation. The front wall needed to be replaced, for what was the purpose in putting on a fresh coat of paint if the walls did not have the strength to survive on their own? As I stood in front of the cabin, I understood that sometimes tearing down was necessary for building up, and in my heart I could see how the campers were faced with this everyday. They too were building back foundations that had been torn down. Their courage and physical abilities had been challenged beyond what any child should experience, and yet amazingly they rebuilt through hope, determination, and youthful exuberance. With their example in mind, it was with excitement that we began to remove the front wall of the cabin.

In the following days, a new cabin began to emerge from the deteriorated structure that once existed. After replacing the front exterior wall with plywood, the cabin held a new ray of hope. As the six new windows were installed, I soon learned the true value of small boards called shims, and a level became my new best friend. After the installation of the windows, additional wiring was done to accommodate a newly purchased light and a window air conditioner. Next, insulation was added and interior plywood was installed. This was followed by floor and ceiling trim and two coats of interior paint. Now my attention turned to the exterior of the cabin. A bleach wash was applied to remove a mold build-up on the rear and sides of the cabin. An exterior trim was added to the windows and door, and a new door and screen were then installed. New prefab concrete steps, two fresh coats of paint, and sod completed the cabin renovation.

As I surveyed the cabin, I reflected on the past days that led to the remodeled structure. While the cabin renovation was once just a goal I saw in the distance, it was now complete. I had discovered that there was no need for fear when stepping out of your boundaries to help someone enjoy life a little more. I quickly learned that others shared my same ambition to assist these children. It was amazing how volunteering became contagious and truly provided a great sense of accomplishment for every individual involved. My early insecurities of construction work were quickly cured by my fellow volunteers' willingness to teach.

The obstacles that would have proved daunting for a single individual became manageable with the assistance of others. When I reflect on how I gained the courage to take on such a project, I realize it came from my first experience as an activity assistant 3 years earlier. Often, individuals with good health feel they are entitled to more; however, these children truly understood that the best part of living was life itself. They looked at every day as a gift and lived each for its own value. Courage is not taught, but it is displayed. These children displayed courage every day and from them I learned its true meaning.

Nicole Fortenberry
Hattiesburg, MS

Nicole Fortenberry is a typical brown-haired, brown-eyed girl living in Hattiesburg, MS, with her mom, Denise; dad, Davey; and sister, Sarah. She was born in Knoxville, TN, on August 21, 1992, but she has since lived in Michigan, Indiana, and finally Mississippi. Nicole maintains an A average and has received numerous awards. She especially enjoys science. She is also a member of Dixie Baptist Church, where she sings in the choir. Her favorite activity is soccer. She was a member of the 2001–2002 Girls All-Star soccer team in Hattiesburg that won the gold and bronze medals at the State Games of Mississippi. She is now a member of the HYSA V-II Select Team. Besides soccer, Nicole is involved in cheerleading, Girls in Action (GAs), choir, basketball, and softball. Nicole is a kind, loving, and thoughtful young girl who is very caring toward others and their needs.

Bear Donations

When I moved to Gulfport, MS, I met Mimi Rowell, the first great influential person in my life outside of my family. She was my first caregiver when my mother began her teaching job. Mimi is one of the sweetest, most caring women I have ever had the pleasure of knowing. She is always there when anyone needs help, especially children. She cared for me and her grandchildren, as well as many foster children, worked in her church, and cared for her neighbors and friends in sickness and in good health. Mimi is the kind of person I want to be.

I am very lucky to have many other great women in my life. My grandmothers are both active in our church, serving on committees, teaching Sunday school, and supporting their church families in any way possible. My mom has always been involved in the church and the community. She has been a Brownie Scout leader, Sunday school teacher, children's church worker, AWANA leader, and a volunteer in school and in community organizations. She is a high school teacher, and I see how much she gives of herself to help her family and students.

Recently, I have begun to look up to Mia Hamm as a great role model. I love soccer, and Mia Hamm is a great player; but, more importantly, she is a great person. She uses her popularity as a soccer star to help raise money for needy kids and also teaches less fortunate kids how to play soccer. I watch Mia make a difference in the lives of others, and I want to do the same.

The September 11 tragedy has changed the way I look at life. I want to make a difference and help make the world a better place in any way I can. But, my feelings of wanting to help started before September 11. As a Brownie Scout, I learned there were people in our area who did not have enough clothes and food. I am blessed to have a home with a mom and dad with plenty of food to eat, clean clothes to wear, and toys. Other children are not so lucky. Our troop decided we wanted to help. We collected food, toys, and clothing for a local shelter. As a GA (Girls in Action) member of my church, I have learned that we can and should help the people living in our own community. We also collected clothes for a family in need, sang carols for the elderly to brighten their Christmas, and collected money for missions. During Sunday school and Vacation Bible School, I learned that it is better to give than to receive. That is what I wanted to do. I wanted to try to get involved, to do more.

It was almost time for my birthday, and we were beginning to plan my party. I had a friend who donated $30 of her own birthday money to help an elderly woman repair her house. I thought I could also use my birthday to help someone else. I asked my parents if they minded if I asked my friends to bring items to donate to a worthy cause instead of giving me gifts at my party. They thought it was a great idea, and we started researching ideas for donations. My mom called the Forrest County Sheriff's Department and told them what I wanted to do and asked if there was anything they needed or if we could be of any help. They said that their corporate sponsor for the "Hug a Bear" program had just informed them that they would not be able to donate teddy bears anymore. The officers use the teddy bears to help kids who are afraid.

That was it! I got really excited. My mom helped me to write my invitations with a teddy bear shape asking each friend to bring one or more new, unwrapped teddy bears to be donated to the "Hug a Bear" program instead of a gift. It was a great success! More than 40 bears were collected for donation.

Even though I didn't receive birthday gifts, this was the best birthday party I had ever had. We had a great time swimming, playing games, and eating, and we all felt great about what we were doing. All my friends said it was one of the best parties they had attended. On the Monday after my party, my dad checked me out of school early and we took the bears to the sheriff's department. Two officers and Rocky, their dog officer, met me. My sister and I had pictures taken with all of the officers, including Rocky, and the teddy bears. Everyone at the sheriff's office was very nice and thanked me for being so thoughtful. I was very happy. A few days later, my dad took some more bears that were donated by the friends who could not come to my party. While he was there, one of the officers told him they had already used one of my donated bears to calm down a little 5-year old girl who had been brought into the station. She was scared and unable to talk. She had seen something bad happen with her parents and the police needed to help her feel better and talk with them. The officer said that she liked the bear and immediately began to feel better. Soon, the little girl was able to talk to the officer about what she saw. I am so glad that I was able to help the little girl and the police. It truly is better to give than to receive.

This has been such a great experience for me. I did not do it for myself, but it has been much more of a positive experience than I could have imagined. I received coverage in our local newspaper and then was recognized again in the editorial section by a kind gentleman. I have gotten a lot of compliments and comments from teachers, friends, and family. I also received a "Good Citizen of the Year" commendation from the Sheriff. I have enjoyed my experience so much that I plan to make the "Hug a Bear" birthday party an annual event. My friends said they had a great time and loved donating to help children. My friends and I are also trying to think of ways to get bear donations during other times of the year. I hope other girls my age think of ways to help kids in their communities. We can all help make things better!

Chelsea Freeland
Charleston, IL

Chelsea Freeland was born on November 21, 1991, in Houston, TX, and currently lives in Charleston, IL, with her mom, dad, and younger brother. Charleston is a small university town with a little more than 10,000 residents, and it was here that Chelsea began performing community service on a regular basis. Chelsea loves art and science, especially geology and paleontology, and she wants to be a scientist. She also enjoys playing clarinet in her school band and is a purple belt in Kempo Jujitsu Karate working toward a black belt. Being persistent, determined, intelligent, and kind is what Chelsea believes makes her a good service leader in the community. Chelsea provides service in order to help others. Her projects focus on educating community members on a variety of subjects including science, community safety, history, and literature.

Planning a Science Fair

I participated in science fairs and won awards in Texas, and it was a positive experience. When I moved to Illinois, my district did not have a science fair. I always liked doing the experiments, and I thought the kids here would enjoy them, as well. Science was always the fun part, but I also enjoyed seeing everyone else's projects. I spoke to teachers about a science fair. They said they used to have them, but stopped because they felt the parents were doing the projects. I decided to plan a science fair and encourage the students to do their own projects.

To begin creating a science fair, I first researched other science fairs from Web sites. I located numerous fairs for a variety of ages that utilized different models. There were many types of judging forms, sets of rules, entry forms, and project suggestions. Using these resources, I created my own entry form, judging criteria, project guidelines, timetable, and methodology information sheet. After the research was completed, I met with Dean Hanner and Associate Dean Obia of the College of Sciences at Eastern Illinois University (EIU). The university agreed to sponsor the fair believing that it was for a good cause. They said EIU would provide a university auditorium, chairs, tables, and funding for copies, a judges' lounge, and other supplies. With the dean's support, it was also easier to ask faculty to judge the fair. Though they offered to buy the trophies, the student organizations needed to be involved, so I asked them to volunteer on fair day and provide the money for trophies. Next, letters were sent to the College of Science faculty asking them to judge and serve on review committees as needed. Many decided to volunteer their time and help out on fair day.

With the university pieces in place, the student information sheets and entry forms had to be prepared. On these handouts, I included a brief summary of the scientific method, types of projects, and fair guidelines. These forms provided project requirements and suggestions, as well as local resources. I urged students to make the project their own. After the handouts were complete, it had to be approved by the district. I met with the assistant superintendent to secure approval so the handouts could be distributed in the public schools. After they were printed, they were bundled into groups by school and classroom and delivered. Then, I waited for replies.

At the entry deadline, I collected the forms and grouped the participants and looked to see which entries needed to be reviewed by chemists, physicists, and such. I contacted faculty for necessary evaluation and then notified those participants of the review decisions. Next, I coordinated the timetable and agenda for fair day. As the students created and experimented, I continued to prepare materials for fair day. I worked with a local trophy company to design the trophies for the winners. I sent reminders to all my volunteers and participants and prepared contestant packets with fair day directions, participation certificates, and pencils. With preparations complete, I awaited the big day.

Registration, the judges' room, and the auditorium were prepared as we waited for everyone to arrive. When the university student volunteers arrived, I trained them to work registration and contestant set-up. When the elementary students arrived, I supervised registration. Once the students had registered and set up their projects, they were dismissed until interviews later in the afternoon. I then welcomed the judges and offered them coffee and muffins in the judges' room. For the judge training session, I went over the rules and judging criteria and shared the student handouts for reference.

After training, the faculty volunteers judged the projects with multiple judges for each project. When the judging was complete, I served lunch to the judges while my assistant (my mother) tabulated the scores. After lunch, I met with participants to prepare them for interviews while my mother trained the judges for the interview session. As part of the initial judging session, I had each judge provide two positive comments and two positive suggestions for each participant. I knew the students would be nervous about interviews and wanted them to return to their projects and find positive notes to put them at ease.

After the final training, the judges returned and ran the interviews and then retreated to the judges' room to decide the winners. When the calculations were complete, we returned to the auditorium full of science fair participants and their friends and families. My mother acted as emcee so I could hand out the trophies. We thanked our volunteers and congratulated our participants on their hard work. Finally, the winners were called and given their trophies. We took pictures for the newspaper and cleaned the rooms.

The science fair gave students an opportunity to enjoy completing science experiments and sharing their demonstrations to university faculty members. The faculty who volunteered their time got to do a fun service project of their own. I learned the importance of organization, how much time and effort is involved in putting together a community activity, and how important it is to work with others. I also learned a lesson in patience and perseverance. Many members of the EIU faculty thought my mother was doing all the work. On fair day, they commented that, as they watched my mother carry boxes and me run the fair, they were sorry they had doubted my efforts.

I encountered some obstacles throughout the experience. Fewer students entered than I expected and even fewer actually showed up. As this was my first experience with a large-scale activity, this may have been a good thing. It was a manageable number of people and that made it easier. Since many students had not seen a science fair before, they did not know what to expect.

The university has decided to hold the science fair again. Hopefully, more students will enter and participate. Since I am not running it, I will be sure to enter. There was a tremendous amount of help from university faculty, administration, student organizations, my parents, local scientists, and business owners. For other young volunteers attempting large projects such as this, I would suggest planning well in advance, understanding that you must follow through with the project once you start, and getting the help you need to be successful.

I began this project because I thought Charleston needed a science fair for elementary students. In the course of the 2-year planning period, I decided to use this experience to earn some Girl Scout awards. More than 200 volunteer hours were acquired in the final year of planning and implementation, and I earned the Girl Scout Junior Leadership Award and Bronze Award. Though these awards only require about 50 hours of service, this project was well worth the extra time.

Through Girl Scouts, I have done several other community service projects on my own. I planned and completed a street cleanup project to educate college students on the effects of their drinking and throwing bottles on neighborhood sidewalks, endangering local pedestrians and our pets. I also held a book giveaway for local elementary teachers. I had a large collection of books below my current reading level and decided they would be better used in classrooms for educational purposes than in my garage. In addition, each summer I volunteer at the local historical society's 1920s ice cream social. I planned children's games from the 1920s to play and conducted a visual presentation of the popular Pilates exercises during this time period. Most recently, I read stories from the *Winnie the Pooh* collection and did a presentation on the author, A. A. Milne. I also offered coloring pages and crayons for the younger visitors because of the popularity of crayons at the turn of the 20th century.

Community service takes time and effort. I continue to plan activities to help my community and better the lives of others and myself. My parents are role models for service, as they both volunteer their time and energy. My female role models include J. K. Rowling, Mia Hamm, Marie Curie, and Sue Hendrickson. They are all women who have displayed determination and perseverance and have followed their dreams. I hope to contribute to society as they have.

Kristen Hadeed
Flagler County, FL

Kristen Hadeed was born in Gainesville, FL, on February 26, 1988, to Al and Maureen Hadeed. At 2 years of age, she moved to Flagler County, FL, where she lives today. Kristen has one younger sister, Lauren. Kristen attends Flagler Palm Coast High School, and she enjoys math, English, and gifted studies. She is involved in many activities and clubs in her community including cheerleading, dance, church youth group, and Community/Future Problem Solving. Kristen loves working with kids and was a volunteer at United Methodist Christian School for 3 years where she worked with babies. She now has a job there. Her hobbies are running, swimming, shopping, and hanging out with her friends. Kristen is an outgoing person who loves to help people. She is a determined, friendly teenager whose goal is to make a difference in the world.

Domestic Violence

Over the past year, I have been involved in a community problem-solving project designed to create awareness of domestic violence. Community Problem Solving is a competitive program where a team of students finds a problem in their community and tries to solve it using creative problem solving skills. The students then compete at state and international levels. This past year, I was on a Community Problem Solving team of 16 students called Students Against Violence—Especially Domestic (S.A.V.E.D.).

Flagler County, where I live, is the fastest growing county in the state of Florida and the eighth fastest growing county in the United States. Such growth has resulted in an increased rate of domestic and school violence. My team's goal was to create community awareness on domestic and school violence so residents of our community would be committed to meeting the needs of the victims and survivors.

We worked with the Family Life Center, our county's shelter for domestic violence victims. We launched a media campaign using the resources of the Family Life Center and Boss Advertising and Design (a local advertising company). We created and printed a brochure about domestic violence that contained information and the abuse hotline numbers. My team also created a skit on domestic violence. This skit was performed at many different events, including a Flagler County School Board meeting and at our county courthouse. It was even recorded on video and sent to a county television show called *Inside Flagler County Schools,* where it was aired. The video was also sent to all schools in our district for students to view.

In October 2001, my team attended a youth summit on school violence held in Orlando, FL. At this summit, we received bookmarks, banners, posters, and T-shirts, which were used in our project. My team laminated the hotline numbers on the bookmarks and distributed them to all of the public schools in our county. Seven thousand of these bookmarks were given to students. We also hung the banners and posters around our school and posted the abuse hotline number throughout our hallways. My team also gained copyright permission to use the slogan of the youth summit, "Silence Hurts, Speak Up and Save a Friend."

In October, which is National Domestic Violence Awareness month, my team created lapel pins that displayed the abuse hotline number. We handed these out to more than 1,000 citizens of our community. We also created pizza box fliers that displayed the abuse hotline number; these were distributed to more than 2,000 residents on Domino's Pizza boxes. Awareness booths were set up at our county's Home Show and at the International Craft Fair, where we distributed brochures, bookmarks, and additional information. The abuse hotline number was also posted on school marquees around our county.

During our county's home show, I was manning my project's booth when an older woman came to me in tears. She told me that it was wonderful that I was doing this project because domestic violence is a big problem in the world. She said that, when she was younger, she had been domestically abused and she had wished there had been a group like ours to help her get out of her situation. It really meant a lot to me. From then on, I was inspired to go on with this project. Whenever someone told me that my project was really making a difference, I knew I had to keep working toward my goal.

In December 2001, our team organized a holiday party for the victims and their families living at the Family Life Center. Gift bags were created for the children, we cooked a holiday feast, and we arranged for Santa to be there to give out presents. This was a very touching and self-fulfilling experience for me because I felt like I gave suffering children and their families a memorable holiday.

Our team was featured in a local magazine, *Palm Coast Living,* in newspaper articles, and on the local news. In April of 2002, we were nominated for the United Way Volusia/Flagler County Youth Group Volunteer of the Year Award by the Family Life Center. We attended the nominee's luncheon and discovered we had won this prestigious award. We also learned that we were being awarded the Point of Light Award and received a letter from the President of the United States.

In addition to these awards, my team received proclamations and resolutions from our local area governments stating that we had made a difference in our community. We met with U.S. Senator Bill Nelson and State Representative Doug Wiles to tell them about our project.

One of the biggest obstacles our group faced was that residents in our community were not aware that domestic and school violence were such big issues. By doing this project, my team planted a seed in the local, state, and national governments. We not only have made the residents of our community aware of domestic violence, but we have created national awareness about the subject. This is an extraordinary accomplishment.

The biggest obstacle I faced was wanting to do more than could be managed. I really wanted to make the issue of domestic violence nonexistent. This, of course, was beyond my ability as a teenager. Creating an awareness campaign was the solution to my problem. By spreading awareness on the subject, I would be making domestic violence a diminishing problem.

Through this project, my team has touched the lives of more than 14,000 people and tripled the service statistics for the Family Life Center, which means that more victims called into the hotline and used their services than ever before. My group was fortunate to win first place at the state competition for Community Problem Solving, and we advanced to the international competition in Connecticut. At this competition, we competed against 3,000 kids from around the world, and we received the honor of winning first place in our age division in the Health and Human Services category.

More than 1,000 community service hours were spent on this project from which I have learned so much. Unfortunately, I learned that there are people in the world who are not very lucky—people who suffer everyday because of hardships in their lives. My goal as a teenager is to make this life better for them and take away their pain. I also learned a lot about domestic violence, which will help me in future relationships. I know now what a healthy relationship is supposed to be like. So, if I am ever involved in an abusive relationship, I will know how to get out of it and get help.

Through this project, I have found many female role models. One of them is my teacher, Mrs. Tomko, who introduced me to Community Problem Solving. She is very active in our community and is always willing to help someone in need. My mom is also one of my role models. At times when I felt like giving up the project, my mom encouraged me to keep going. She reminded me of what I was accomplishing and how many people I was affecting. Fortunately, I have the opportunity to do another Community Problem Solving project. I am working with another group of students to create Breast Cancer awareness in our community. We're also going to comfort cancer patients going through treatments by giving them care bags and performing random acts of kindness. I hope that, this project touches many more lives and impacts positively on my community and the world.

One of the best things a person can do for the world is to volunteer in his or her own community. Even though times may get rough and sometimes you feel like giving up, stick to your morals and believe in yourself. Just think of how many people will be affected by your kindness—this alone will get you through.

Michael Renee Harp
Forest City, AR

Other than a year and a half spent in Georgia as a small child, Michael Renee Harp has lived in Forrest City, AR, all of her life. She was born on December 5, 1986, and has been raised as an only child in a single-parent household since her parents separated in 1989. Michael has enjoyed participation in all the arts through 4-H, church youth groups, Girl Scouts, and independent study. She has received various awards in dance and painting and also enjoyed band until she began homeschooling in 2000. Michael Renee has participated in many service projects in Forrest City and throughout St. Francis County over the years. Most of her service opportunities stemmed from her Girl Scout membership. She has also found opportunities for serving others through her own initiative.

Busy Hands—Blooming Heart

I have been involved in community service for quite a while. It began with planting trees at a local elementary school when I was 6 years old and has continued ever since. Some of the service activities were easy, and some were more difficult, like designing and creating an indoor fish pond. Some were pretty time-consuming, too, such as making decorative birdhouses and then delivering them to lots of different homes. All the projects in which I have been involved have been enriching, interesting learning experiences. I once received recognition for my efforts from the Prudential Spirit of Community Awards Program, which was a pleasant surprise. My past projects have included handing out pamphlets for and having discussions about voter awareness, annual participation in the National Park cleanup, home visits with the terminally ill, annual caroling for the elderly and disabled who are unable to get out of their house much, donating artwork to retirement homes, making coloring books for the kids at St. Jude Children's Hospital, enhancement projects at retirement homes, and dance demonstrations for the elderly.

I was also a volunteer at the Special Olympics, and it was one of the best experiences I have ever had. I was rather surprised by the number of local competitors that kept coming up to me over the next few weeks. It was all very touching; not only their excitement, but also that they had remembered me.

One of the most enriching projects was having craft classes for the elderly at a local retirement home. Preparing everything and then making the crafts took about 2 hours every Saturday for 4 months. Some things turned out great, others were not so good, but we always had fun. The participants would tell me all about themselves and always wanted to know what was going on in my life. I was 10 minutes late one time and they were all worried that something had happened and that I was not coming. On the last day, we had a little party. It was fun, but a little sad, too. We all cried and hugged each other. About a year after the project, a son of one of the participants told me that his mother still talked about me. That was a little surprising, but it made me feel good, as if I had really done something worthwhile.

My most recent project is volunteering with Adopt-A-Platoon. I send weekly e-mails and monthly care packages to troops in Kosovo and Afghanistan. I think they really need to know that we appreciate what they are doing over there, and that we are thinking about them. This entire project has been very educational and enriching. I don't know where they find the time, but the military men and women send really informative letters describing what things are like there with lots of pictures of themselves and the areas in which they are stationed. The varying conditions on the different bases around the world are also very interesting.

I am currently working on starting a new project that will assist victims of natural disasters. This project is going to take a bit of work, but looks as if it will be very fulfilling. I have been First Aid and CPR certified and will be working directly with victims after a disaster. I doubt that it will be necessary for me to use my new skills, but you never know. It seems that, no matter how many volunteers there are at a location, they could still use more help. I just hope the people I work with are helped in some way—that they are made more comfortable and know that there are people who care about their plight even if they don't know them personally.

I started getting involved in service projects because of my mom; things like this are important to her and she has taught me the value of helping. There are so many lessons to be learned from every service activity. When you go into something not thinking about getting anything in return, you always find that your life is touched and changed by the very people you are trying to help. When I planted that first tree, I never thought I was going to learn so much or be so blessed by doing nice things for others.

Most service projects don't require a lot of preparation, just the "getting out and doing it" part. Convincing yourself to do something is the first step. You have to look around and find a need that you feel you are able to help with, and then you come up with a plan of action. After you review your plan, you have to be sure that it is not too big for you to handle or you will need to find others to get involved and help. You don't want to feel pressured to get something done by a certain time or be so busy during the project that you don't have time to really experience the good parts.

My mother is always in the background, so I guess I get any needed boosts of courage from knowing that she is there just in case I need her help. Most of the time, I only need help with travel and unloading any supplies I might be using. I guess the most important thing I have learned from all of this is that it actually requires very little of me and the rewards from those lives I touch are so great. Your life is changed for the better, and forever, when you spend just a small amount of time helping others.

My nanna and my mom are my role models. They have both raised children on their own, which I think must take a lot of courage and strength. They also do lots of things for others in the community, even though they are sometimes very busy just doing their own stuff. My mom is sometimes discouraged by how much she needs to do and how little time she has. She tends to feel guilty about dirty dishes and a messy house when I think that is really pretty unimportant compared to some of the other things she is busy doing.

I think everyone should try some sort of service project. Everyone can do something, and every little thing makes a difference. I have grown in more ways than one, but with my physical growth, I have been able to take on more complex projects.

Laura Haskell
Cleveland, OH

Laura Haskell was born on September 21, 1984. She attended high school at Hathaway Brown School and loved being a part of the all-girl environment the school provided because it brought out her full potential as a student. While at Hathaway Brown, she was an active member in the dance program and was involved with the rest of her dance class in helping senior citizens at a local nursing home express themselves through movement. She lives in the community of Gates Mills with her parents, Anna Kay and Jim, and her brother, John. In her spare time, Laura enjoys babysitting, baking, dancing, playing with her baby cousin, Molly, and spending time with the elderly. She is responsible, compassionate, and respectful, and she absolutely loves to talk and interact with people of all ages and abilities. These qualities make her a great volunteer.

Helping the Elderly

I was 12 and about to enter the seventh grade. I had nothing on my mind but spending my lazy summer days relaxing by the pool hanging out with my friends. The fact that my brother, John, was going down to an adult daycare center, Parma Hospital's Elder Center South, 3 days a week had no impact on me whatsoever. That is, until he started telling me exactly what he was doing there. His stories first started out as the sarcastic, "Yeah, I hang out with old people." Eventually, he began to reveal how the participants would tell him about their lives—living through wars and the Great Depression and how they would give him their valued bingo prizes because they appreciated his being there so much. I began to see a change in my brother; he had a different outlook on life. He had a new-found respect for the elderly and for himself. I wanted that change and sense of fulfillment.

The next summer, I enrolled as a candy striper and volunteered at the same center. My first days of volunteering were quite unnerving. What would I say? How would I act? I was around so many people with different stages of dementia, Alzheimer's disease, and mental disabilities that it was quite intimidating. I had never been around people in situations like this before, and I certainly did not know how to respond to them. The staff was very understanding about the way I felt, and they explained to me that I should just talk to the participants as I would with anyone else. Slowly, but surely, throughout my first summer there, I became more accustomed and comfortable. Now, I am able to relate to these people as I would with my friends and family. In fact, they have really become my friends and family.

When I first began volunteering at Parma Hospital's Elder Center South, I would ride my bike 2 miles, 3 days a week to get there and work for about 3 hours a day. However, a few years later, we moved to the east side of

Cleveland, so I could no longer ride my bike to the center. I then had to drive about 45 minutes to get there. Progressively, I increased the time spent at the center, eventually spending 5 to 8 hours a day, 3 to 5 days a week. Unfortunately, due to increased demands at school, I was only able to spend my summers volunteering. During my senior year, however, I was able to go to the center 2 or 3 days a week. Although it is not as much time as I am used to spending during the summers, I feel quite lucky that I am able to go there at all.

When I volunteer, I do a multitude of different things. I listen to the participants if they want to talk to me. Sometimes, all they need is to be listened to, and it is often hard for them to find someone with enough patience to just listen. I also take part in a variety of games and activities with them. Some of these include bingo, balloon volleyball, sing-a-longs, painting, or even holding tapioca rebellions!

Although I do take part in many participant-oriented activities, a large portion of what I do with my time while volunteering is working in the kitchen. Most people do not understand why I would want to do this, so I will try my best to explain. The way that I define volunteering is giving up my time to help others. If I can take care of the tedious kitchen work, it leaves so much more time for the nurses and the aids to spend with the participants, giving them much needed help and attention. It also relieves a lot of the stress and tension so the staff can go about doing more important things. If there is less stress and tension, it allows for a much happier and calmer environment for everyone. I do not mind doing dishes if I know people in the long run are benefiting from it.

I do not even know where to begin expressing how much I have learned and grown from my volunteer work. I have learned to love and accept people for who they are. I know not to judge people based on their looks or behaviors, and I have learned the fine art of patience—knowing that all people move, grow, learn, and develop at their own pace. Most importantly, I have learned the great fulfillment of giving my time to others. I cannot stress enough the feeling I have knowing I am doing something selfless, and the fact that I enjoy it so much is truly rewarding. The people I have met at this amazing facility have touched my heart in ways that are inexpressible. When I walk in and see shining, smiling faces, and waving hands from people who appreciate my being there, I feel something I cannot possibly begin to express. I do not continue spending my time at the center for the feeling that I get from it. I volunteer because I see how happy it makes so many people and that is what makes me so happy. It is definitely a win-win situation.

Whenever I see Mary's bright face telling me about her weekend, dear little Katie asking me when it will be Halloween, or Craig, who is always the first to embrace me in a warm hug, I cannot help but feel lucky to know these amazing people. I also feel fortunate to be able to volunteer with the staff that works there. They, too, are all remarkable individuals with an enormous amount of love to share. I do not know if I would have been able to have this passion for volunteering with the elderly if not for them. They have taught and guided me, and for that I will always be grateful.

Volunteering is an amazing thing. I have truly loved every minute of it. Soon, with the rest of my dance class, I will take part in a service opportunity with a local nursing home to help the residents learn the art of movement. I am a somewhat serious dance student, so with this project, I will be able to combine two things that are very special to me: my love of working with the elderly and my love for dance.

I would encourage anyone and everyone to volunteer. Even if it is only one day a month, give your time and energy to a worthy cause. It is undoubtedly worth it. My time spent with people so different from me has helped me to grow as a person. I hope to continue doing volunteer work throughout my college experience and my life. It is a break from all the stress and business going on in my life. It gives me an escape and the chance to sit down and talk to someone with different experiences. I give much of the credit for my success in volunteering to my brother because, without him and his stories, I may never have become a volunteer. Volunteering will always and forever have a special place in my heart.

Amanda Hickman
Ooltewah, TN

On May 19, 1985, Amanda Hickman was born to Carl and Cheryl Hickman. Amanda was raised north of Chattanooga, TN. She attends Ooltewah High School, where she spends on average 40 hours per week participating in a myriad of extracurricular, school, and community service activities ranging from science fairs, to youth legislature, to the marching band. Her favorite subject, chemistry, is also her intended college major. Amanda's pursuit of academic excellence and school service has taken her from editor of the school Web site, class officer, and Model United Nations head delegate to the chairman of the superintendent's student advisory council and a member of the school board representing more than 50,000 students in Hamilton County. Amanda's dedication to excellence, coupled with a desire to serve her fellow students, defines her as an outstanding, positive activist.

Amplifying Student Voice

I will never forget one special day in fifth grade. For an entire year I had dreamed of serving on the safety patrol. I vividly recall sitting in the auditorium, holding my breath, and hoping my name would be called, and at last it was. I was thrilled. I made my way to the stage and received my badge. The rest of that year I patrolled hallways, helped younger students, and assisted in the cafeteria. As a result, I realized that you did not have to be famous or an adult to make a difference. Anyone can change things by taking action.

In middle school, I honed my skills as a speaker, leader, and activist for change. I worked diligently on my speaking skills, realizing that, by communicating your opinions, ideas, and solutions, change could take place. I participated in several oratorical contests, winning second in the nation in the seventh grade. I was also a 3-year member of the student council. The student body expressed an interest in homecoming activities that particular year. As a new school, there were no homecoming events, no pep rallies, and very little student participation. As the student council president, I campaigned for these activities by meeting with teachers and principals. These meetings were successful, and that year the school had its first pep rally, schoolwide class competitions, and spirit events during homecoming. I dedicated myself to transforming the role of student council president from a figurehead to the position of an advocate for students with the responsibility for scheduling activities, planning meetings, and organizing community service. I acquired many of the skills that would contribute to my future success, including leadership, organization, time management, and teamwork.

These attributes have proven to be the foundation for my success in high school as an activist for student rights and voice in policy. The lessons I learned gave me the strength and courage to pursue my endeavors. I held my first high school office in 10th grade serving as French club president. That same year, I became a member of the high school marching band leadership group and a Ruri-Teens officer (a service organization that concentrates on patriotism and community involvement). In all of these positions, I endorsed student leadership and command of activities.

Also during the 10th grade, I fell in love with chemistry. I delighted over atomic structure and was thrilled by stoichiometry (the quantitative study of chemical changes). Toward the end of the semester, I applied for acceptance to the Governor's School for the Sciences at the University of Tennessee at Knoxville. On the application it asked if I had taken Chemistry II or Advanced Placement Chemistry. At the time, I was unaware these classes were offered in high schools. The next day, I went to my chemistry teacher and asked if our school offered a Chemistry II course. He replied that our guidance department would not implement the class. I knew the course would be beneficial to my success in chemistry, in college, and beyond. This became my first challenge.

I was determined to convince the guidance department to offer a Chemistry II course for the population of students who displayed an interest in the sciences. I began my campaign by scheduling a meeting with the 11th grade guidance counselor and an assistant principal. They set forth the following requirements: a certified teacher willing to teach the course, a minimum of 15 students registering to take the course, and approval by the science department chair. My goal was to secure these requirements. My chemistry teacher was interested in teaching the course and had taught it previously at another school, and the science chair welcomed the opportunity to broaden the spectrum of the science curriculum. I then visited current chemistry and physics teachers requesting lists of students who might be interested in and capable of taking the course. I personally contacted each of these students and explained the course and the potential opportunity available. I also connected with the intellectually gifted case manager at the school and provided her with the information to distribute to students during their individual educational program meetings. At the end of the year, 20 students had registered to take the course, thus all three requirements were met. The next year, Chemistry II was offered for the first time in more than 3 years at my high school. The program has continued to grow and was offered again the next year.

After this experience, I realized there was not a palpable voice for students in most schools, including my own. My 11th grade year, I ran for class representative to the student council, where I began petitioning for student rights. I met with principals in a positive and respectful manner about student complaints concerning an array of issues from school food, to the effectiveness of study hall periods. I served on our school Carnegie Grant Team as a representative for students on issues of school flexibility, structure, and curriculum. I was able to use the skills I had obtained in middle school to reach the administrators and create change.

In my junior year, I also became the editor of the school Web site, where I worked to personalize it for students. By working individually with teachers, I assisted them in the creation of classroom Web sites that allowed students to access homework, study guides, review material, and enrichment activities related to the curriculum. Although I am no longer the editor of the Web site, it continues to grow and more teachers every week are learning how to use the Internet to supplement their classrooms. I continue to work with teachers in my spare time to strengthen this program even today.

That same year, two other students and I were nominated by the administration and faculty of my school to serve on the Hamilton County Superintendent's Student Advisory Council. In this position, I was able to meet once a week with three students from each of the 17 high schools, Hamilton County Department of Education employees, and the superintendent of schools. The role of the council was to provide a connection between students and the superintendent. At each meeting, a question-and-answer session with the superintendent and his staff was held. During my first year of service, I lobbied for a wheelchair accessible ramp at my school. One of our disabled students approached me with her need for a ramp in the front of the building. She had been calling the county office requesting the ramp, but had seen no results. I discussed the issue with the superintendent and one of his assistants at several of our meetings until a ramp was finally built at my high school to provide access for all of our students. I also lobbied for gifted education funding, a reduction in out-of-class standardized testing, and the reinstatement of out-of-state field trips after September 11. I sought out those with the power to create change, presented the issue, and found they were willing to listen and help.

At the end of my first year serving on this advisory council, I was elected as the chairman and thus the student member of the Hamilton County School Board. In this role, I have already begun to plan a student forum for the Hamilton County Schools. Most recently, I worked along with a steering committee comprised of the superintendent, members of his staff, area principals, teachers, and, most importantly, students, to plan the first annual Student Speak-Out Forum. Five ambassadors from each high school were invited to meet and discuss issues that are most pressing to them. Soon, I will present the opinions of the participating students to the school board. This year, the Superintendent's Student Advisory Council will also begin a middle school adoption program. High school students will be assigned to visit area middle school student councils and then represent their voices at our monthly meetings. I am also researching the effects of new curriculum paths on students of different academic strengths and extracurricular interests, as well as serving on the Tennessee Student Congress on Policies in Education as the second vice-president.

Throughout the past 7 years, I have learned that activism is simply recognizing a need and then providing the microphone to express that need to others. I was blessed with wonderful parents, as well as outstanding teachers and mentors who desired to assist me in my journey through school. However, I recognized there were others around me who were less fortunate. Providing a voice for those people has been and continues to be my goal. I have learned that there is a solution to every problem; it may take patience and compromise to find that solution, but it does exist. The most essential part of activism is being willing to take the first step and turn a solution into a reality.

Lizzie Horvitz
Shaker Hts., OH

Lizzie Horvitz was born on January 11, 1988, and currently lives in Shaker Heights, OH. She has a sister who is in college. Her mom and dad are both close to her and like doing service-related projects, as well. They are involved at the Cleveland Museum of Art, the Cleveland School of the Arts, as well as many other civic institutions. Lizzie plays lacrosse, tennis, and squash, and she is interested in the performing arts. She also likes being with friends and doing service-related activities. Lizzie's favorite subjects are English, theater, and chorus. She has many reasons for doing service. It makes her feel good and she feels that she has accomplished something by tutoring children or feeding the hungry. It would feel much worse for Lizzie to just sit there and know that there are people she could be helping. Instead, she does something about it, and that makes her feel good.

Preparation, Action, Reflection, and Celebration

In seventh grade, I was active in the Service Learning Club. Service learning is different from community service. Community service is going out and helping people, but not really knowing why you are doing it. Service learning has four major components: preparation, action, reflection, and celebration. The first component, preparation, is when you are introduced to concepts of service learning and discuss community issues. Action involves going out in the community and actually doing the service project. Reflection is talking about how you feel after you have completed your service project. Finally, celebration is when students are recognized for the great things they have done. I think service learning is more meaningful because people explore what they are doing and why.

During my 2 years as a service learning member, I went to the Collinwood Food Bank, the Sunbeam School to tutor children, and other places. I spoke at the Empty Bowls banquet about my experience, and throughout the year I helped get others involved. At the Empty Bowls banquet, we told our guests what we had been doing all year. Our topic was hunger. The Empty Bowls banquet is a perfect example of practicing the four components of service learning. There are two ways to look at it. The first was when we prepared for the banquet by brainstorming what we should talk about and what we wanted to accomplish. Next, we acted by making sure we were ready to hold the banquet. We had to send invitations, write speeches, and make sure everything would be perfect. Reflection was the actual banquet, where we could think about all we had done throughout the year and then celebrate our accomplishments. Another way to look at the four components in a broader way is where the banquet was our actual celebration. First, we learned about hunger and prepared to go to the food banks and soup kitchens, then we went and helped the people, next we talked about each individual aspect of our actions, and, finally, we celebrated by holding an Empty Bowls banquet. At the banquet, we told everyone our stories and experiences at the soup kitchens and food banks. When everyone was leaving, they received a bowl we made so they would remember that there were hungry people who needed help. Empty Bowls was a success, and it made everyone feel happy that they had worked so hard all year.

In eighth grade, I was elected president of the Service Learning Club for the middle school of Hathaway Brown. There were three other officers leading the middle school in service learning projects. Half of our job was to go and make a difference, as service people were supposed to do. The other half of our job was to raise awareness and get others involved. I feel that I was successful in my tasks. I knew from the beginning that, by joining the Service Learning Club, I could not end world hunger or teach every illiterate person in the world to read, but I knew I could make a difference. I faced many obstacles on the way. One of them was sharing a leadership role with three other classmates. It was a good experience, but it wasn't easy. As expected, we did not agree all the time. We all thought we knew what was best. After much discussion, we finally reached consensus and overcame the hardest obstacle of all. We decided to have literacy be our main topic. My three other leaders thought it would be best to have a few main topics such as literacy, hunger, and helping the victims of September 11. We finally figured out that it would be smarter to approach this opportunity by focusing on one topic, doing a wonderful job, and helping a lot of people instead of tackling a variety of topics, doing a pretty good job, and only helping a few people. We went to Sunbeam every week to tutor children ages 7 and up. Some the kids we tutored were our age or older. It was a great experience, and not only did the kids get something out of it, but I got a lot out of it, as well. It made me realize how lucky I am and how good it feels to help people and give something back. One of my favorite experiences at Sunbeam occurred on one of my last days there. My favorite little boy was reading a book to me. As I corrected him, he was thankful, but I could tell he was getting frustrated. He kept reading and making mistakes here and there. At the end of the period, I told him we were through, and he said to me with a straight face, "Thanks, Lizzie, I think you've helped me to be a better reader." That was the moment when I knew what I was doing at Sunbeam was worthwhile, and I realized that I was not only helping myself, but helping others, as well.

From the experience of doing a year of service learning and being the president, I learned that service learning is a lifelong project. I thought that I could overcome anything in a year, but the truth was I could not. We could only help a small percentage of the population here in Cleveland, and as much as it paid off, I felt bad that I could not help more people. It also was troubling to see how much help some people needed. As bad as I felt, I could only feel more and more happiness knowing that I had made a difference in a child's life. I was not alone, either. There were many people who helped me along the way. Teachers and my parents helped a lot with my stress level, planning, getting in touch with those whom I needed to reach, and building my confidence. There were times when I felt that I couldn't make any more of a difference because I was only 14, but my teachers and parents convinced me that even a kid like me could make a difference to someone somewhere.

I would have to say my female role models are anyone who does anything service-related in their everyday life as a job. Whether it be individuals who work at a soup kitchen or who teach at an underprivileged school, they dedicate their lives to helping others. They are giving, helping, and not self-centered. That is the kind of person that I strive to be everyday.

I think that television and books got me involved. I would watch these commercials about Christian Children's Center and I would read about how people were going hungry every day and read statistics about individuals who were not as fortunate. I felt that it was my place to let others know what it's like to have the same opportunities as others.

When I am older, I want to be someone who cares about others and shows it. Sure, it looks good to other people, but that's not why I want to be that person. I want to aspire to be that kind of person because I will always know that I made the right choice in what I decided to do with my life. I want to help others, which is one of the most important things anyone could ever do.

Meredith Kirsch
Pompton Plains, NJ

Meredith Kirsch thrives on activity. Born on September 23, 1986, she is the youngest of three children and resides with her parents and older brother and sister. Meredith is a student at Pequannock Township High School, where she takes part in numerous activities. In the fall, she plays the clarinet for her school's marching band, and winter finds her on the basketball court. Since Spanish is her favorite subject, Meredith is active in the Spanish Club and serves on the club council. In addition, she is a Future Business Leaders of America member and has demonstrated her acting skills in her school's one-act drama competition. She is also a senior Girl Scout and is currently working toward the highest honor, the Gold Award. Meredith has a passion for using her skills to help others. She has been engaged in leadership and activism for years and reaps satisfaction from her volunteer work.

The United Nations and Beyond

I became aware of the potential for children to help other children after hearing a fellow teenager speak about the horrors of child labor and exploitation. His organization, Free the Children (FTC), is an international organization founded and run by youth to benefit children of the world. I was so moved that I immediately volunteered at the local FTC chapter and subsequently was elected its director while in the eighth grade. With my leadership, our local chapter has organized car washes, dances, and other benefits to provide for the needs of poor children locally and beyond our borders. Overall, we have raised more than $10,000 as kids helped other kids.

Since the start of my involvement in the reformation of child labor and child rights, I have taken part in many eye-opening experiences. As a 14-year-old, I attended a conference held at the United Nations regarding the issue of children in armed conflict. That same year, I participated in an international youth conference in Toronto, Canada, meeting youth from around the world, living and learning together, and honing our skills to become successful leaders of youth.

One of the most important skills I have gained through these experiences is effective public speaking. For the past 3 years, I have been writing speeches and giving presentations about the realities of child labor, poverty, my involvement with Free the Children, and, most importantly, the power of one. I have spoken at numerous schools, places of worship, youth groups, and colleges such as Ithaca College, The College of St. Elizabeth, and The New School in New York City. I feel a strong need to inform others about the truths of today's society and to empower young people to make a difference.

How did this all begin? Well, some people say that I want to save the world. I accept the challenge. I truly believe in the power of one: the ability one individual has to make a difference. Throughout my upbringing, my parents have always encouraged me to recognize and share my talents with others. Christian service was an everyday occurrence at my elementary school. My experiences in Girl Scouts extended the idea of service to others. My older brother and sister were role models, and I eagerly followed their examples in volunteering.

A turning point in my life was when I heard that teenager speak passionately about the issue of poverty and child labor. This sparked the desire in me to help in the crusade to change the world. I felt empowered to initiate the change I wanted to see. My first activities were small, attending Free the Children meetings and helping with projects. My family's support provided me with the encouragement to get involved. As I learned more about the organization, I assumed greater roles in the chapter, first as secretary and then as director. The night high school students voted me, then an eighth grader, as director of the chapter was when I realized my greater potential. Those teens encouraged me to be a risk taker and to lead them. My parents and siblings offered their love and help. I gained confidence from my peers and support from my family. I had the courage to lead. As time went on, I realized that my passion to help others was raised to a new level as the leader of a youth group. Not only could I help needy children, but I could also help my peers realize their potential.

Over the past few years and through my efforts in FTC, I have networked with youth around the globe as we tackled multiple issues to benefit the needy. As a member of Free the Children, I had been asked to serve on the International Youth Board, which is a panel of young people from around the world who make decisions and vote on Free the Children policies. Meetings were held over the Internet, and my eyes were opened to different cultures as I met people

from different countries. It was through this work that I met
Fintan Kilbride, a retired Canadian teacher. Each year he
takes students from around the world to work with the poor
in Jamaica. After hearing him share his poignant experiences, I decided to travel to Jamaica and see firsthand the
things of which he spoke.

The first step to traveling to Jamaica was to inform my
family. To my excitement, my brother and sister were also
intrigued and expressed an interest in going on the trip.
Needless to say, my parents had questions about sending
their children to a Third World environment for 2 weeks,
but I was determined to go. After we researched the country,
my parents were finally convinced that we would be safe. I
then began saving money and preparing for my adventure. I
contacted civic groups seeking donations toward my trip.
My brother, sister, and I gave presentations and collected
funds that way. A year passed from the time I had first met
Fintan to when I found myself saying goodbye to my comfortable home life and boarding an airplane on my way to a
new and extremely different place.

I lived like the poor in Montego Bay and Kingston,
Jamaica, for 2 weeks in the month of July. While there, our
group spent long, sweltering days teaching reading,
Spanish, and math at summer schools. We also played with
and took care of babies at an orphanage and spent time
with lepers at a home for the abandoned elderly. The people with whom we worked had nothing. They were the
poorest of the poor, and, just as they did, I went to bed
hungry every night.

In preparation for my journey, I collected items from
home to give to the people in Jamaica. I collected small toys,
books, clothing and school supplies. At the end of the 2
weeks, I distributed the items among the different centers. I,
along with many others, gave the shirts off our own backs to
help these families. I came away richer.

My trip to Jamaica is one that will certainly never be forgotten. It opened my eyes to so many aspects of my everyday life that I would normally have overlooked. By comparing my life to the lives of others, I realized how fortunate I am. Unfortunately, poverty plays a large role in the world today, and a great deal of suffering takes place because of it. I have learned that this poverty is not necessary and can be changed. I have learned that, many times, political issues have an impact on social issues, and the women and children of the world are often the first to suffer.

I now have a better understanding of how our world economy works. The differences between First and Third World countries are much more evident to me. Visiting Jamaica has made me consider my future. I hope to continue to educate myself on global issues and do all that is possible to aid people in need, both locally and abroad. My horizons have been broadened, and I will always take with me the things I learned and experienced in Jamaica.

I am passionate. I am empowered. I am a leader. When I reflect on all my experiences, I value the importance of the events that have impacted my life in such a positive way. My life has spiraled from first becoming an avid supporter on a local level, to leading on a local level, and then networking and affecting the world. I have faced challenges and have worked hard. I have seen the results of collaboration and of sweat. I would do it all again. I will do more.

How did a quiet girl get to the United Nations and beyond? She followed in the footsteps of the women in her life who lived as leaders. My mother is active in Girl Scouts and is a successful school principal. She manages the household effectively. Through her example, she has taught me to think, love, and follow my dreams. My older sister has had just as important an impact. With 4 years between us, she has had the maturity to guide and teach me life skills. I watched as she pursued her passions, and she encouraged me to do the same, but to be my own person.

I truly believe in the power of one. I have seen how one person can make a monumental difference in the lives of others. My advice to other girls is to recognize your talents and your passions. Research, speak out, and take action. The smallest good deed is greater than the best intention left undone.

Lauriel Marger
Englewood Cliffs, NJ

Lauriel Harte Marger was born February 19, 1993, and lives in New Jersey with her mom; her dog, Biscotti; her cat, Rocky; and her guinea pig, Babe. She has incredible comedic timing and wit, which she uses as a volunteer "humor ambassador." Besides helping sick kids and making grown-ups laugh, Lauriel loves diving, playing her flute, and going to Broadway shows, museums, and her synagogue. She also enjoys hanging out with her pets, making up dances with her friends, and traveling. Lauriel participates in orchestra, student council, safety patrol, and Girl Scouts. Her favorite subjects are science, art, writing, and reading. She enjoys helping people and animals and doesn't realize how extraordinary her charitable activities are for her young age. Lauriel is compassionate, considerate, determined, imaginative, logical, honest, and able to resolve conflicts.

Not Just Clowning Around

My charity work began when I was 5. Instead of getting presents at my Chanukah party, I asked everyone to bring a children's video to donate to the Englewood Hospital pediatric floor. It was really fun delivering them to the children. I couldn't think of anything else I wanted, and it just seemed like I had too much already. It dawned on me to do a video drive after I had gone to the hospital for a medical test. It didn't seem like there was a lot to do there, so I thought watching videos would be a good idea. The head of the department wrote me a thank-you letter letting me know how happy the patients were to have some entertainment.

In kindergarten, my mom and I started our Daisy Troop with two other families. As a scout, we do service projects for the local senior facility and the town nature center, among other activities. I like to raise awareness and money for animal charities since I would like to be a vet someday. In the past, I have gone to the local shelter to walk the dogs in order to give them exercise and attention. Since I love to draw, I participate in two local art events: one to raise money for Cystic Fibrosis and one to raise awareness for fire safety. I actually won a ribbon for my fire poster one year. Through my student council activities, we raise money for different causes each year. It allows me to meet many kids from other grades, too.

My biggest charity commitment happened when I was 6 and my mom got cancer. For some reason, she thought that I was very funny. Silly things I did made her laugh while she was having surgeries and going to doctors' appointments. She thought that everyone should have the opportunity to laugh each day for free. She realized that many patients do not have a funny 6-year-old around to help them find joy, so she began a charity called The ComedyCures Foundation. In a way, I was destined to do lots of charity work.

I helped her pick the ComedyCures charity logo and assisted in designing the brochure and lots of other details to launch the charity. I actually helped her start all of the different programs because they came from our everyday life. For example, I made my mom a *Get Well Joke Book* after her surgery. She loved my handmade gift. Now people all over the country make them for patients because my mom loved hers so much that she started a charitable Joke Book Program. Now, there are even life-sized, bilingual joke books bringing joy in children's hospitals. I told my mom silly jokes when I was little, and now there is a 24-hour LaughLine so that patients across the country can call (888) Ha-Ha-Ha-Ha to hear or donate a silly joke. I still record a joke sometimes, too. Kids and grown-ups have called the LaughLine from 43 states and Canada.

The best part of my charity work is when I go with the comics to camps for sick kids. We show people how to use laughter for wellness. We put on funny clothes and do silly skits to make them laugh and have some joy. We do shows with many different professional comics and improv actors at schools, Gilda's Clubs (cancer support clubs for women, named after Gilda Radner), senior centers, and hospitals.

I go to the auditions and work with the actors. If they can make me laugh, then they are usually selected because we need comics who can work with kids. Then, we all meet to rehearse, and I help them make up the skits. We usually invite the audience to be in the shows, so the skits have to be kid-friendly, too. I help buy different props and costumes for our programs. I also give out the gifts after our programs to the participants. Sometimes, we do big health fairs to teach people about the importance of therapeutic humor and laughter, and I pass out thousands of brochures while wearing a funny hat and a Humor Ambassador T-shirt.

I get my courage from my mom (she's a single mom and a cancer survivor). Also, knowing that I have given less-fortunate kids some joy makes me feel really good about my contribution. I have learned that people who are sick aren't that different. For example, when I went to Paul Newman's camp for sick kids, most of the kids looked just like the kids in my class. These kids were up on the rope courses, yet they still had to take medicine and go to the doctor a lot.

I have realized that I have a great life and there are kids less fortunate than I am. Serving other people is fun, and sometimes I get to meet famous comedians. Meeting TV and newspaper reporters is exciting, too. Some obstacles to my volunteering are that I miss some of the shows for ill children at the special camps when I go to my own summer camp. My mom can't take me out of school to do programs like she did in the beginning because the charity is just too busy. I can only do nighttime and weekend programs. Sometimes, I get nervous, but I just look at the other comics and gain confidence and inspiration. Participating in the charity is both fun and rewarding.

My favorite living role models are Holly Knorr, a veterinarian from Animal Planet's *Emergency Vets*, my mom, and Jane Goodall. Clara Barton, Eleanor Roosevelt, Amelia Earhart, and Annie Oakley have inspired me, too.

I've learned a lot from volunteering that I may not have learned at such an early age. It's important to know you can tell the press that a question is too personal. Also, even though I'm a little person, I can still make a difference in the world and so can you! I've seen that volunteering is as easy as making an ill person smile or recording a joke. I'm actually thinking of starting my own animal charity because animals mean everything to me.

Amanda Napier
Petal, MS

Amanda Napier lives in Petal, MS. She was born on July 4, 1988, in Hattiesburg, MS. Her parents are Judy Napier and the late Mac Napier. She has attended Seminary Elementary School and Ocean Springs Middle School, and is currently a student at Petal High School. She likes to read and write short stories, has two dogs and one cat, tutors classmates, and is a member of the Petal High School Band, student council, beta club, and photography club. Her favorite subjects include English, math, and French. Her patience with and concern for people and animals have resulted in various types of volunteer work, including work at Southern Pines Animal Shelter, United Blood Services, and Forrest General Hospital. Amanda is an outgoing person who enjoys life. She especially loves volunteering at the animal shelter and plans a career in veterinary medicine.

Lessons Learned From the Animals

I volunteer at three organizations in Hattiesburg, MS: Forrest General Hospital, the United Blood Services, and the Southern Pines Animal Shelter. Although I enjoy volunteering at all three, my favorite is definitely the animal shelter. As long as I can remember, animals have surrounded me. I have owned a wide variety of pets—everything from goats, horses, dogs, cats, and hamsters, to rats, turtles, fish, guinea pigs, and rabbits. One of my earliest memories is of someone asking what I wanted to be when I "grew up" and responding, "I want to be an animal doctor!" I haven't changed my mind since.

I first became interested in volunteering at an animal shelter after seeing a flyer requesting volunteers for the Gulfport Animal Shelter when I was visiting the Ocean Springs Library. Imagine my disappointment when I found out there was an age requirement of 13, and I had just turned 12. The next year, after moving to Petal, I decided to check with the local animal shelter, hoping they would need a volunteer. I was in luck. On my first Saturday during the drive to the animal shelter, Mom tried to explain a few things to me. She gave me a stern lecture about how I was not to ask for any of the animals, no matter how cute or adorable they may be. I promised not to, but I've broken that promise more than a few times. She warned me not to be upset if they had to euthanize an animal, but her attempt to prepare me was futile.

When I arrived at the animal shelter, two employees greeted me. They were patient and showed me how to clean the cat cages, spray out the puppy kennels, replace dirty blankets for the younger puppies, sweep and mop the floor, wash the animals scheduled to go home, and deal with people coming in to look at the animals. My first day working at the animal shelter was an interesting experience. I succeeded in dropping a cat bowl and spilling water everywhere, putting the wrong kittens together in the wrong cage, and giving all the cats an inappropriate amount of food. Luckily, no permanent damage was done. I soon learned the routine and felt like I'd been there forever. I realized quickly that there was no use trying *not* to become attached to the animals. They are irresistible, and I love them all.

Volunteering at the animal shelter has provided me with many valuable lessons and experiences, some positive and others negative. The positives far outweigh the negatives. Following through on my commitments is a very positive experience. I've made a commitment to be there every Saturday, and being dependable is important to me. Another good experience has been working with other people. Even though I'm the youngest and we're all different, it's great how we work together to take care of the animals. Two other lessons learned are how to follow instructions and, just as important, time management. It's easy to run out of hours in a day and, occasionally, even days in a week. With the demands of high school band, homework, and volunteering at three different places, time management is essential. A negative side to working at the shelter is witnessing the evidence of animal abuse. There are people who prefer not to own a pet, but I didn't realize there are those who would deliberately mistreat and abuse animals. I'll never forget the Saturday that a beautiful Labrador retriever had been severely burned because his owner had poured hot grease on him as punishment. Knowing that all the animals can't be taken home is heartbreaking. Seeing them each week, with some still there week after week, it's impossible not to become attached to them. Sometimes, I feel like I have 1,003 pets. The most valuable lesson learned from the experience of volunteering is how to accept gratitude. Working at the animal shelter helps the employees and the animals, and I'm glad to know that my work is appreciated.

I have gained many benefits from volunteering at the animal shelter. I get a wonderful feeling knowing that I've helped an animal. My ability to influence and educate people about animals gives me a sense of accomplishment. I love asking people to spay and neuter their pets and having a good explanation to give them about why it is so important. In addition, I've encouraged several of my friends to become interested in volunteering, and I've learned a lot about animal behavior.

I have encountered few obstacles while volunteering. It's been difficult giving up my Saturdays. With high school being packed with so much homework and so much time spent out of the classroom on schoolwork, it is difficult for me to give up that one day of rest and relaxation. However, I'm so glad that I did decide to work at the animal shelter because helping the animals is more rewarding than sleeping late. Another obstacle has been realizing that not every dog and cat is nice. There are some that are aggressive, mean, and will bite. It's been hard, but I think I've finally accepted that, though most animals are nice once you get to know them, some animals just can't be handled. People tend to think of animals as cute little mounds of fur providing entertainment; however, each has its own personality and deserves to be treated with respect.

I would definitely repeat my volunteering experience because working at the shelter is a wonderful part of my life. Something invaluable is learned every week, and I highly recommend that others participate in any type of volunteer work. There is a sense of satisfaction that is gained by helping others that cannot be found elsewhere.

Elina Onitskansky
Cleveland, OH

On May 14, 1984, Elina Onitskansky was born in Odessa, Ukraine. When she was 6, her family moved to Cleveland, OH, where she first attended Agnon School and later Hathaway Brown School. Ever since she was little, Elina loved school, especially math, science, and history. However, she also found activities outside of school fulfilling. Elina first began volunteering when she was in fourth grade and continues today. She has found that charitable work and positive activism are rewarding activities. Since her first volunteer job, Elina has volunteered in nursing homes, schools, shelters, benefit races, and anywhere else help is needed. She realized that she could express her caring nature and also benefit from the interaction she had with others through volunteering. Elina is currently attending Harvard University.

The Elderly and Oral History

Volunteering and positive activism have undoubtedly changed my life in ways I could have never imagined. My community service and activism have allowed me to enrich my life in countless ways by enriching the lives of others.

As an idealist and a caring individual, I have always wanted to improve the world, both at large and around me—volunteer work and activism allowed me to do just that. I began volunteering when I was in fourth grade. The whole experience began rather casually. My friend's big sister volunteered in an area nursing home, so my friend and I decided to visit and see what it was like. That summer, I only volunteered 18 hours, but that time was enough for me to realize what a positive and unique experience volunteering really is. As I talked with the residents, I began to understand that, even if they were not physically or even mentally fit, they were amazing people. Most of them were kind, generous, and loving, and they absolutely loved interacting with children.

I also began to realize what an unbelievable opportunity I had to talk with people who had lived through so much and who, therefore, had so much wisdom and experience to share. I am a history buff, and I love to learn about the past and to participate in current political affairs. Talking with the residents, I realized they had lived through the history I was studying. I spoke with people who had been soldiers, Holocaust survivors, first female college students, and so much more. Each resident had so many life experiences to share with me. Sometimes, I felt like I was gaining more from the experience than they were. Yet, I knew they appreciated my work as a volunteer, and my volunteering took on new meaning because of the personal connection I was able to make with many of the residents. As I got to know them more, I began to understand how much of a positive influence a volunteer can have, and this encouraged me to continue volunteering.

As a teen, it's hard to imagine being elderly, and while there can be much satisfaction in reaching a "ripe old age," there can also be many disappointing and trying times. Sometimes, though, it's the little things that can make the biggest difference—a smile, a friendly ear, a companion to walk with, someone with whom to visit the store, play a game of Scrabble or Bingo, or sit with over a bowl of ice cream. As a volunteer, I was able to do all of these simple things for the residents that make their lives just a little brighter.

For these and many other reasons, I found volunteering intensely satisfying, so I continued doing it year after year, and I found myself quite naturally increasing the time I volunteered. I also began to try different volunteering jobs. At first, I had only worked with the residents helping with their daily activities, but then I became involved in helping with special programs, such as those for holidays. Each new activity taught me something more. Through my volunteer work, I also got the opportunity to meet other amazing people who were also volunteering.

I found the whole experience so satisfying that I wanted to share it with others. In eighth grade, when I was offered the position of junior volunteer coordinator, I took it gladly. This position was highly fulfilling in that it allowed me to share my love of volunteering with others, but it was also extremely challenging.

As the coordinator, I had several responsibilities. I had to orient new volunteers, arrange for volunteering jobs, place the various volunteers in the jobs that suited them best, help them interact with the residents and staff, monitor their progress to ensure that they were having a positive experience, take care of much of the daily office work related to the junior volunteers, and plan the junior volunteer party for the more than 70 people. At the same time, I realized there were some things missing in the program, so I also decided to create my own junior volunteer handbook and develop some new and unique programs, such as "Adopt-a-Grandparent."

Sometimes, being the coordinator was rather difficult. If a junior volunteer was not following the rules, I found myself acting as the "bad guy" to my peers, and this was always difficult. Being a coordinator and planning events was also difficult in that it involved many skills that I did not have at first. I kept at it and learned something new from every mistake. I loved the position because it allowed me to help new volunteers discover the benefits of volunteering; but, at the same time, I often found the job demanding. While I was acting as the junior volunteer coordinator in grades 8 through 12, I was also trying to live a normal high school life, which involved school, homework, extracurricular activities, and down time with friends. Sometimes, it felt like everything just wouldn't fit. But, volunteering was important to me, so I made it fit. This involved creative time management, like getting up earlier than most of my friends. As a rule, when something is as fulfilling as volunteering was for me, you make time for it. Somehow I managed to do the activities I loved, hang out with friends, and still have time for volunteering. In fact, I began to volunteer even more. I found other volunteer work at the Food Bank, as a tutor, and on the Democratic Coordinated Campaign. Slowly, as my views matured, I also realized that there are ways, in addition to volunteering, by which one can improve the community. One of those ways is positive activism. I learned a little about activism through my work on the Democratic Coordinated Campaign, but I got my real taste of it the summer before my senior year.

My junior year, I became concerned with many of my peers' blasé attitudes toward the Holocaust and the Japanese internment camps. In response to that concern, I began to do some research concerning these events. Through that research, I found some amazing information on the Danish rescue of the Jews. The Danes rescued 97% of their Jewish population as opposed to the 33% of the general European Jewish population that survived the Holocaust. I was immediately fascinated. Finding a lack of information on the subject, I decided to research it. That was easier said than done. For one thing, I knew that I wanted to do an oral history of the Danish rescue, but I was unsure of exactly how to conduct such a study. So, I began looking for information.

First, I took out books on the event and on oral history in general, and I learned from them. I also asked my teachers for guidance. They were able to help me by allowing me to apply to become a Strnad Fellow. At the same time, I began to contact various Jewish historians in the area. I hoped that one of them would be willing to mentor me. Fortunately, I found an amazing mentor. She was able to share much of her experience with me, which was very helpful. Unfortunately, she was also busy, which meant that I still had to get much of the work done on my own. However, her guidance allowed me to clarify the processes I would have to go through while doing this project. I quickly realized that, in order to conduct this oral history, I would have to travel to Denmark, which was rather expensive. My school was able to partially support me as was my family, but I still had to do a lot of independent fundraising, which I found was different and much more difficult than fundraising as part of a group. I also discovered that it was difficult to convince people that I, as a high school student, could really conduct this oral history and write a book. Slowly, I was able to garner support from some members of my community.

I have learned through my activities that, if you want something bad enough and are willing to work at it, sooner or later (often later) you will be able to get things to work. Finally, with the help of my school, my mentor, and some members of my community, I traveled to Denmark and interviewed several members of the Danish Resistance. I quickly realized that, even with the intense preparation I had done for these interviews, I was not as prepared as I would have liked. Being an oral historian is hard. I had to learn to be the camera crew, the interviewer, and the attentive listener all at the same time, and it was not an easy task. But, the amazing people I met and the unique and fascinating stories they had to share made it all worthwhile. Their courage, daring, and ingenuity will inspire me and hopefully others for years to come. From their incredible stories, I wrote a book entitled *A Lesson in Humanity: The Rescue of Danish Jewry.* This was also a difficult and time-consuming task, which I was doing at a time when I had at least 20 other things I needed to be doing. But, it was important to me; I was passionate about it, so I kept working on it.

Volunteering and positive activism have changed my life in so many ways. Time and again, in trying to help my community, I met amazing people who have enriched my life in so many ways. Remember, "Volunteers are not paid, not because they are worthless, but because they are priceless."

Caitlin Patterson
Cleveland, OH

Caitlin was born on October 22, 1987, in New York. At age 4, she moved to Seattle, WA. At age 5, she moved back to Cleveland, where she currently lives with her parents and younger sister, Nell. She attends Hathaway Brown School. She plays field hockey and lacrosse and is a member of the swim team. She has been a member of the Service Learning Club and was the grant officer for the student-run foundation at her middle school. She is a very good student. Her favorite subjects are history and science because she loves learning about the past and asking questions. On weekends, she loves to hang out with her friends. Ever since second grade, Caitlin has been involved in community service with her church, family, or school. She is a girl with a big heart and a determined mind. She always goes the extra mile to help someone and has the ability to motivate others to help out, as well. In the future, Caitlin plans to use her leadership skills to create positive change in the world.

Bringing Light Into Sunbeam

Although I have participated in many service learning projects throughout my life, nothing has touched me more than working with the kids at Sunbeam School. Sunbeam, a Cleveland City school, is designed to meet the educational needs for a variety of students. Two thirds of the students at Sunbeam are either orthopedically handicapped or otherwise impaired. All of the students at Sunbeam live below the poverty line.

I attend a small, private, academically rigorous school for girls. In the seventh grade, my classmates and I were given the opportunity through the Service Learning Club to partner with Sunbeam School. We went to Sunbeam once a week for two periods and helped in the classrooms. Only about four or five girls volunteered to do this. I thought this would be a great opportunity because it would give me a chance to teach, which I love to do, and it also would give me a chance to help our community. One of the kids I help could even end up finding a cure for AIDS, because I helped him or her learn to read and inspired him or her to help others.

I have also been involved in our middle school student-run foundation, G.R.O.W. (Girls Reaching Others Worldwide). The G.R.O.W. foundation's mission is to award grants to schools or organizations for service learning. During the first year of the foundation, one teacher and three girls wrote the bylaws and the mission statement, receiving a $750 grant to begin their work. The second year was focused on fundraising, and more than $5,000 was raised with one grant awarded. During the third year, focus was given to getting the word out to other schools and organizations about our foundation. Although fundraising was continued, our main goal was to publicize the foundation through brochures and presentations and accept proposals and award grants. While serving on the foundation, we raised more than $4,000 and awarded approximately $1,500 in grants. One year, I was given the opportunity to be the grant officer, which meant that I would oversee the decision-making process of whether or not to award grants to organizations who applied to our foundation. After working on the foundation, I wanted to get some hands-on experience and help out in the community myself.

On my first bus ride to Sunbeam, my teacher asked us our thoughts and expectations regarding Sunbeam. When first asked this question, I had no idea what I thought about the experience I might have. But, as the trip went on, I began forming a picture in my mind of what I thought this school was going to look like. The picture in my mind was of a dark, scary school with dirty kids who looked like they had not eaten in weeks. I expected the school to be in a small alley with trashcans up and down the street.

When we arrived at Sunbeam School, I received a big slap in the face. I found a nice school on a pleasant street with flowers growing outside and children laughing. As our small group walked into the school, we looked around and felt a bit awkward and out of place. This was a new experience for most of us. The school was brightly lit with student artwork hanging on the walls. There were classrooms to our left and a small pool to the right. Groups of students passed by us, some in wheelchairs and others walking. All of the kids were welcoming and waved to us.

We met with the head of the school, who told us where we were going to assist. I helped out in a room full of 12- and 13-year-olds. At first, the kids were nervous to talk to us, just as we were to talk to them. They were welcoming, but shy. I was supposed to help with a group of four boys. I didn't know what boys were like as learners because I had been in an all girls school and had never interacted with boys in the classroom. But, I took the challenge and worked hard to get through to them. We were reading *Maniac Magee*. I had already read this book, which was a relief to me. We had to read a chapter and take turns answering questions. At the end of the day, I was sad to leave and told the kids I would be back next week.

After that first day at Sunbeam, I was hooked! I continued the relationship with the Sunbeam School throughout my seventh- and eighth- grade years. Sunbeam became my favorite part of the week. I couldn't wait to see the students and teachers I had grown to love. The goal of our program was to build a relationship with a certain teacher and class. The teacher I formed a relationship with was one of the coolest women I have ever met. She could have done anything she wanted—become a doctor or lawyer, even the President—but because of her love for helping kids, she became a teacher. She loved her students and took great care of them. She would think of fun games for them to play during the period instead of just lecturing to them.

Once, we played a game where she set up sheets of paper all around the room. Each student had to write a thought on one of the sheets of paper. Then, she gave the students 5 minutes to go around the room and reflect on the thoughts their classmates had written. This was an interesting way to have a discussion. Instead of just throwing out an idea and having them discuss it verbally, she had them communicate through writing. She and I became closer every week. By the end of the year, I was very sad to say goodbye.

Over the year, I developed a special relationship with one particular girl. I was paired with her to help with her reading. This girl had cerebral palsy and was in a wheelchair. Even though she had these physical disabilities, she was very intelligent. It was hard for her to read out loud, so she would read to herself as I read along with her. If she had trouble, she would ask for help. We read books about kids our own age going through the hardships of slavery. Although we didn't communicate much verbally, I felt a connection with her because we both loved to read so much.

Throughout the summer, I tried to figure out a way to extend my relationship with the Sunbeam students as I entered high school. I met with a few of my teachers and talked to the head of the Sunbeam School. One of my teachers told me about an upper school program called the Student Research Program. This program is designed to let students be involved in research outside of school for the entire 4 years of high school. Many students have been working on science research in medical labs. I thought that this program might be the perfect way to combine my love for science and my relationship with Sunbeam School. My hope is that I will be able to design and complete an educational research project that will benefit children like the kids at Sunbeam. Then, not only will my experience with Sunbeam benefit me and the kids with whom I directly worked, but possibly all children who are orthopedically disabled.

When people ask me where I got the inspiration and courage to enter into a new relationship with people who appear different than me, I tell them it is from my parents. Service to others has always been part of my family's beliefs. My father is a doctor at a county hospital, where he takes care of many low-income families, and my mother volunteers at our church and my school. My first taste of community service was working side by side with my mother and my sister in a Christmas soup kitchen. Anytime there is a call for donating money, toys, clothes, or food, I am the first to donate. I think this is because I believe that to whom much is given, much is expected.

Brooke Rinehart
Asheville, NC

Brooke Rinehart was born on April 24, 1989, in Asheville, NC, where she has lived all her life. Brooke's parents are Gerald and Sandra Rinehart. She has a brother, Kyle. Brooke has many interests, including volleyball, basketball, softball, skiing, running, going to church, hanging out with her friends, helping other people, and just spending time with her family. She has visited nursing homes, singing to the men and women there, and has been a part of Operation Christmas and many more charitable activities. Brooke is involved in the academically/intellectually gifted program, student body council, Beta Club, FCA, athletics, and her youth group. Her favorite subject is math because it comes so naturally to her, and she has had many awesome teachers who have made math interesting. She has been involved with a math competition called MathCounts. She is a great philanthropist because she gives so much of herself. She gets along with people, respects everyone as equals, and thinks that, no matter who you are or how old you are, you can make a difference in this world. Her life verse is "Don't let anyone think less of you because you are young."

Dream It, Believe It, Achieve It

It all started when I wanted to become president of the Enka Middle School student body council. I wanted to help make a difference in my peers' lives. Our school had just finished being under construction for about a year. Nobody had any pride in our school because, for the past year, it had been a wreck. There was trash all over the place. Bathrooms were not clean and nobody cared about our school anymore. So, I thought about how we could get back some pride in our school if I should win my election. I wanted to make an impact.

Then, it came to me. We could plant flowers, shrubs, and trees around the school to make it look nicer and make it look more like a new school. I also wanted to show the teachers that we appreciate everything they do. When I got elected, I went to my advisor, Mrs. Robinson, and my principal, Ms. Collier, and told them my ideas. They thought about it and decided to let me pursue my project. As a result, I started a school beautification project entitled Enka Jet Pride Plant Day. I did not anticipate all that was to come out of it.

First, I secured donations of potpourri to make the teachers' bathrooms smell nicer. I also acquired soap for the bathrooms so they could wash their hands and feel clean. In addition, we made little notes for the teachers that said, "Take time to stop and smell the roses. Student body council appreciates our teachers and staff." We put the notes on the potpourri balls that we made for the restrooms.

I started writing, calling, and visiting local businesses to see if they would help donate things for our school's needs. I only got a couple of donations at first. Then, the first big donation was received: Home Depot donated $200 worth of plants, plus the assistance of their plant specialist. We were so excited to receive this donation. It was just what we needed to get our project underway. The donation from Home

Depot gave us other ideas. Our PTA president and I wrote a letter to a new housing development and asked for a donation. Anything they could provide would be appreciated. The man in charge called me one evening and said that he would love to help, but first he needed to talk to the head administrator of Biltmore Lake. He called back later in the week and informed me that they would donate $3,000 to our school beautification project. I was so amazed that I could hardly speak to thank him for his generosity.

With this renewed spirit, we called people left and right, trying to get volunteers to come and be a part of our community project. Sometimes, I would start to think that we would not be able to pull it off. That's when everyone helped me. I was encouraged by God, my fellow peers, my family, and teachers. They all helped me through it. When I went into the school to work on the project and to update everyone on how it was going, I would have teachers tell me how good of a job I was doing. It really helped me through the tough times to think of the encouraging things people said.

The Enka Jet Pride Plant Day just kept inching its way closer and closer. We worried we wouldn't have enough volunteers to plant all the flowers and that we would not have all the necessary tools. Finally, the day came. There were so many people who came that I didn't even know who some of them were. We had such a wide range of volunteers from students, parents, grandparents, community leaders, and teachers. They all came out and rolled up their sleeves. It was a blessing to be able to do something so terrific. We worked from 8 a.m. until 5 p.m. It was a long day, but well worth it. Everyone worked hard and worked together. We all had fun and were tired; but, when we finished, we were rejoicing.

While we were planting our flowers, we discovered a proclamation from Governor Easley. It was called Trees of Strength. This proclamation is a reminder of the men and women who serve and die to protect our country's freedom everyday. We planted two dogwood trees for Trees of Strength. We also placed plaques on the trees that will forever stand and memorialize the loss of the lives on September 11, 2001 and in honor of the men and women who protect the freedom of our country everyday.

On September 11, I decided to have a program of dedication in remembrance of the brave men and women who lost their lives. I called local firefighters, police, sheriffs, Army, Navy, Air Force, and Marines. Our Enka High School ROTC came and presented the flags. I received a letter from Governor Easley thanking me for being a part of Trees of Strength. It gave me a sense of healing and peace to help people involved in this tragedy. The program touched everyone. We had the firefighters, teachers, and students crying. My big brother said, "I was choked up not only by the program, but because my little sister was up there, and I was full of pride."

I think that the most important thing I learned from what I have done is that, no matter how old you are, who you are, where you are from, or if you are rich or poor—you can make a difference in the world. Now, we all have pride in our school. We pick up our trash and throw it away because we care. I have pride in myself for what I have done, because I know I have made a positive difference in other people's lives, not just in mine.

I would organize another Enka Jet Pride Plant Day and September 11 program again because I believe these were great opportunities to give of ourselves to improve students' attitudes about our school. It gives me a great feeling to be able to help make positive changes in other people's lives.

My female role model is my mom because she is so strong. She had cancer when I was little and she fought hard for her life and finally gained it back. My mom is back to her normal self. She is my best friend and has made me want to be a better person just because I saw how hard it was for her to be sick. I wanted to do something good to make this world a better place.

My advice to other girls and women out there is this: Try to make a difference in this world. A whole lot of little things make a big thing grow and become better. I pray that you will stand strong for what you believe in. Be yourself. Make a difference and make it good.

Rachel Salzer
Rootstown, OH

Rachel Salzer was born in Akron, OH, on April 4, 1984. She later moved to the small community of Rootstown as an only child residing with her parents and pets. Rachel attended Rootstown schools and graduated valedictorian of her class in May 2002. In high school, she was active in school government and other academic organizations, served as editor of the yearbook, and participated in Danceline (a dance team that is part of the high school marching band) and other functions. Rachel is now attending the University of Akron, where her interests inspire her to try "a little of a lot" instead of experiencing "a few." However, one true interest has driven her from childhood: her devotion to animal rights and welfare. She dedicates her talents to improving life for those who can't speak for themselves, utilizing education, awareness, hands-on experience, and direct aid to achieve her goals. Rachel has received numerous awards and is the recipient of scholarships granted in recognition of her work.

For Those Who Cannot Speak for Themselves

My life as a volunteer began at the age of 3. It was the holiday season. While attending church services, my mother and I encountered an elderly woman talking about her sister who resided in the local nursing home. She was going to pay her sister a visit, remarking how sad this time of year was for those who had no one to come visit them and extend holiday wishes. Though I truly did not comprehend the scope of this dilemma, I did feel something was just not right. So, my mom decided to let me see for myself. We baked boxes of cookies and placed small gifts in each box. We then visited the nursing home and distributed our goodies to eager and appreciative residents. The visit went so well, we signed up to continue the project. Eventually, after hearing the stories of homes left and pets missed, we made arrangements to bring a puppy on our weekly visits. The puppy was secured from the local animal shelter.

As time went on and we made weekly stops at the shelter to select the visiting pup, I noticed there was a tremendous need to aid the throwaways at the shelter. The existing building was a rundown concrete block structure, cold in winter and sweltering in summer. Inadequate plumbing and poor ventilation did not supply proper housing. While the animals rescued were far better off there than abandoned, abused, neglected, or tortured, they certainly were not in humane conditions. I began donating my allowance to the animal shelter for little comforts and began begging to volunteer at the shelter. But, the age limit was 14, and I was only 11.

I refused to be ignored because I had a calling. I think I wore the staff of the shelter down. At last, they allowed me to "try" to complete projects. I surprised them with reliable and consistent attendance and dedication. For a year, I cleaned cages, toted bags of food, exercised the animals, and worked to improve their socialization skills. I did all this in hopes of a second chance being given to these victims of man's inhumanity. I hoped for loads of adoptions into caring homes. For a year, I listened to the problems stated by the board and workers at the shelter. They had a lot of "if only" wishes and no solutions. That's when I decided to take action.

I proposed dozens of fundraising ideas. And each of them met with "That will never work'" or "We have tried that and it doesn't make any money." But, the day I was told, "You are a sweet kid. But, you are a kid, and a kid can't do anything," was the day I went to work. I held my first official fundraiser selling chocolate bars. After 2 months, I handed the shelter a check for $1,400. It was then that I began to attend board meetings. I heard of plans that were years old regarding a new shelter. The cost would be $400,000. While the adults dismissed the goal as impossible, I dedicated myself to reaching the proposed sum needed. I organized a celebrity auction and cleared more than $10,000. A second auction would follow a year later. I sold cookbooks door to door. I set up an ornament tree and made it an annual event. I worked fair booths to spread the word and collect funds. I made public addresses and received donations for the shelter. I worked with elementary schools to inspire projects conducted by classrooms bringing much needed supplies and dollars to the shelter. My personal efforts totaled more than $75,000. But, a major effort on my part was to serve as the honorary chair for the county campaign raising funds for the new building. The goal, due to increased building costs, rose to $750,000.

I must note that, due to differences in the direction the new shelter would take, I resigned from shelter duties. At the time of my departure, $600,000 was banked and directed to the construction of the new building. The new shelter became a reality with a holiday move made in

December 2002. I am delighted that the helpless victims of society's ignorance and cruelty have proper housing and supplies to maintain them as they are offered a second chance at life.

But, my exit from the shelter did not end my work. I discovered a rather unique situation less than a mile down the road from the old shelter site. Happy Trails Farm Animal Sanctuary, a one-of-a-kind facility in the region, offers alternatives to slaughter or euthanasia of farm animals. Here, shelter, medical care, nourishment, and socializing are offered to large animals that otherwise would die of abuse, neglect, abandonment, or cruelty. With funds, animals destined for slaughter are purchased. Many are by-products of drug-related procedures. With time and hard work, these animals can offer their human counterparts companionship, recreation, or the opportunity to educate others in animal welfare issues. They are also excellent stories to illustrate the relationship of humans to the other species with which we share this Earth. They illustrate the unfortunate link of cruelty expressed to animals being transferable to fellow humans, too. There is knowledge to be gained and shared while working in the stalls and coops.

One year ago, the facility consisted of a rundown garage with makeshift stalls and a handful of coops constructed of old wood. Funds were badly needed to supply proper shelter and feed. Medical costs, always a major financial issue, kept the owner from construction. That is when I went to work. I organized a golf outing, sold Christmas ornaments, made public presentations, and organized a craft table at the fall festival to obtain monies for materials. Working booths and advertising the need for labor, I have assisted weekend warriors in the construction of a 14-stall barn complete with a loft, pig housing for more than 25 farm hogs and pot belly pigs, and warm coops with water facilities for fowl. We are also beneficiaries of supply donations from local feed mills and farmers within the community. Local vets serve the medical needs of our animals at cost or for free.

I pursued this work for one reason: There was a need. I made no preparation, for you can never be ready for the situations you find yourself in or the conditions inflicted on the animal. In my case, I approach the animal with a "first do no harm" attitude and then allow my heart to guide my actions. It does not take courage to assist a fellow creature in need. It only takes compassion. I have discovered that I can do anything I set my mind to. I am a living example that a kid *can* and, in my case, *will* contribute. Age is truly irrelevant in acts of kindness. The lesson I continue to learn is that there are good and bad people in this world. I cannot make up for the suffering of those bent on cruelty, but I can relieve some of it. My motto from the beginning of my work has been and remains "I cannot save them all, but each one I do save is a positive in a very negative situation." With the continued support of my parents and many others who now believe, my efforts will continue.

I have been instrumental in the establishment of a new county shelter and new constructions at Happy Trails. My work continues to fund further needs at the sanctuary. My parents, the community, politicians, community groups, and celebrities have aided me. So long as there is a need, I will be there. If one person can be stopped from abusing an animal, one life saved, or one child taught kindness, my work will be worth it.

My mother is my primary source of inspiration and example to follow. She taught me love and allowed me to express it to others and endless pets. Also noteworthy is Annette Fisher, who walked away from a profitable bridal business to rescue and care for helpless victims of cruelty, her annual income now zero. Both of these women have placed the value of compassion beyond a monetary amount.

To any young woman with a cause, I would say, "Go for it." There is nothing stopping you but you. Follow your dreams. Believe in yourself. You are the difference between your dream being just a dream and one coming to life.

Sara Shaaban
Evanston, IL

Sara was born on July 11, 1991, in Singapore. In 1998, she moved to Chicago with her mom and her little brother, Ryan. She likes piano, ballet, and creative and interesting projects and ideas. Sara now lives in Evanston, IL, which is similar to living in Asia because there is a mixture of many different people, cultures, and ideas. She has been many places and has seen a lot of people in need. Sara knows that her music makes people happy, and she enjoys sharing it with others. She can also use her talent in music to raise money toward the education of children. Education is very important to Sara because it lets each person see the world and become a better person.

Making a Difference With Music

Since coming to the United States, I've thought about how I can help the community. I have a lot of music in my heart, and I know that music is my gift and I can use my talent in this area to make a difference.

Through music, I have raised enough money to build a school in Indonesia. Having lived in Asia, I realized that there were not enough schools to educate all of the children in some areas. Education is extremely important for every child, no matter where he or she lives. I asked my mom how to achieve my goal of building a school. She told me to use my musical gift and she would help me find places to share my music. I have played my compositions in churches, nursing homes, for company meetings, parties, and at school events.

Many people have helped me in my community (e.g., my school principal, our local and state representatives) by letting me play for their group. When others hear me play, they ask me to make up a song for them or play at one of their functions. With so many songs, I recorded my first CD, called *Suite Dreams,* just in time for my 11th birthday. We give away the CDs so others can relax to the music, and we also sell copies. The money earned through sales is used to purchase additional books and materials for schools. I have learned that it takes time to raise enough money to build a school. It took me 3 years to raise enough for this school, but building the school is just the beginning.

I also help my local community. I like to draw, and last Christmas I won an art contest for a peace card. I donated the $150 award to the Rice Children's Home, located just five blocks from my house. I have only one parent now, and I thought about what it must be like for children who don't have any parents—this is why I wanted to help these children. I have played piano for the 34 children who live in this home and asked the company who awarded me with the monetary prize from the art contest to donate extra art materials to these children. Since then, the company has donated more than 12 large boxes of art markers, pencils, and paint.

The children are happy with their new art therapy department and enjoy having creative ways to express themselves. Many of the children can't talk about their problems, but creating art is a start to communication. It helps children to be understood so adults can help them. Can you imagine not having a family or a place to live of your own? These children don't, so playing the piano and getting art supplies for an art therapy department makes them happy, if only for a little while, and it makes me happy, too.

People who live in my neighborhood need help, as well. I play games with Mr. Rene, my 92-year-old neighbor, and I check on him when his family is away. Together we do gardening and yard work when the weather is nice. I also bring him little treats that I bake with my mom. He likes this very much. I also rake leaves and shovel snow in the winter for my neighbor Mr. Gary, who is in a wheelchair and has difficulty getting around. Sometimes, I just like to sit with these older people and listen to their stories. They have a lot to say and don't have many people willing to listen. To me, this is meaningful volunteer time even though no one else really knows about it except my family. Sometimes, these small things are the best way to help others.

I am lucky to live in a place that allows me to meet and interact with really interesting people. I have met Coretta Scott King, and she told me to live my dreams and always be a lady. Our state representative is Julie Hamos. I gave her my music and she asked me to come to her presentations and play the piano. She is a woman who has worked hard to create positive change for all people, from newborn babies, to older citizens. She inspires me with all that she has accomplished during her three terms in office. Alice Waters is a chef and the owner of Chez Panisse restaurant in

California. I liked talking with her at our local farmer's market this summer and then having breakfast with her, because she is a woman ahead of her time. She thought about the nutritional value of fresh food, right from the garden to the tables in her restaurant, before anyone was interested.

I think many people have dreams of what they can do. My biggest lesson of all is "Think of what you have to offer and just do it!" Remember—children can accomplish things that really do help others. I worked on raising money for my school project at 8 years of age and completed this goal when I was 10 years old. You may need the help of adults, but a child's idea can have a great impact if you are patient, caring, and keep going. Music comes to me for a reason, so that I can give it out to the world. It comes back to me because my music makes people happy and lets me help them. What's important is what you do with your life—to have respect for yourself and others, to be appreciative, and to be generous. There are so many great ideas in this world and so many needs that people have. If you ask yourself "What do I do best?," you will have your answer just like I did.

Meagan Tidwell
Pontotoc, MS

Meagan Tidwell was born on February 11, 1988, and is the daughter of Stephen and Lisa Tidwell. She has one sister, Morgan. She lives in Pontotoc, MS. She is a member of the Beta Club, band, and flag line. Meagan maintains an A average. She enjoys riding and showing Spotted Tennessee Walking Horses and spending time with friends and family. She is outgoing, energetic, and eager to learn and help others. Meagan has been active in her community through her Girl Scout troop for 9 years. They have done several different community service projects, including a memory garden for students of the community who have died, flag ceremonies, and helping with younger Girl Scouts.

Breast Cancer Awareness

One Monday afternoon, I went to my normal Girl Scout meeting. While there, my troop leader said that she had some important news about an event that was coming up. She also said that not only would it be a great experience, it would help us achieve our Silver Award. We sat and listened with great curiosity. She explained that we had been asked by the head office to help with Race For the Cure since our Silver Award Project was based on Breast Cancer Awareness. My leader said that it would be hard work, but it would be rewarding. Little did we know just how hard it would be, but we were all excited and eager to help. Our troop leader told us to meet at the mall at 7 o'clock the next Monday to stuff goody bags.

The following week, we met at the mall as planned, ate supper, and then the work began. We went to the store that was sponsoring the race, and we saw hundreds of boxes filled with goodies. We were amazed! Soon, we were told what we were to do. We learned that we had to fill 5,000 goody bags to be given out the day of the race. We started right away. We planned how we were going to fill them, and we decided that it would be easiest to make an assembly line. We had more boxes than we had people, so some of us were doing three or four things. We were slow at first, but we finally got the hang of it and became much faster. That night, we stuffed around 1,000 bags. We worked three more nights before completing this task.

A couple of weeks later, it was time for the big race. We were all really pumped and ready to go. When we arrived, we saw hundreds of people preparing. We then realized what we were a part of—a tribute to the victims of breast cancer. Some participants were wearing pink shirts and hats—they were the survivors of breast cancer. Others had signs attached to their back that said "In memory of." Some of us were running in the race and had to get ready and help manage our booth. Our troop had also helped advertise and recruit participants for the race. Our troop goal was to sign up 50 new participants, but our final total was 75. We were so excited! We had worked hard to get people involved and had received support from our parents because they had taken time out of their busy schedules to run the booth while we participated in the race.

When it was announced that it was time for the race to begin, most of the girls in my troop lined up at the front. Then, we anxiously awaited the gun to be fired. When we heard the loud shot, we were off. Some of the girls stayed up front, but some slowed down. I was with the group that stayed in front. When we got tired, we slowed down to a jog. We kept on going, encouraging each other as the people on the sidelines cheered us on. We finally saw the finish line growing nearer. We were almost finished. We used our final burst of energy to cross the finish line. We had completed the race! Then, we sat down and waited for the others to finish. After we were all across the finish line, we took a minute to catch our breath. We had made a plan and stuck to it. If given the chance, we would all agree to do this again because of the feeling we had knowing that we had helped other people. We learned perseverance, teamwork, and organization, but it didn't stop there. We still had to plan and carry out our Silver Award Project.

We planned to have a mother-daughter day in which you could come and learn about breast cancer. We decided to have doctors and nurses talk about breast cancer, as well as some survivors of breast cancer.

Through my work with Girl Scouts, I have become a better person. I have learned to care about others and respect their thoughts and opinions. I have also learned to put others first. Being in Girl Scouts has helped me learn about commitment. Once I say I am going to do something for someone or volunteer to help out with an event, I have to do it no matter what because others are counting on me. My troop gets asked to do many things such as flag ceremonies, registration days, and a lot of other projects because people know that, when we say we will do something, we will do it well. As a result, our troop has earned a good reputation in the community.

The girls in my troop are like a big family. When we are having a hard time, we help each other out. We encourage each other to always do our best. It is not always perfect, and we do have to work hard for a lot of what we receive. It is like mini-lessons for life. This has prepared me for the real world. I have learned to manage my time, acquired organizational skills and creativity, and have become more open. Participating in the troop has also helped me with public speaking and writing.

My family has helped tremendously by just being there and getting me to and from all the places I need to go. They also sign up to help with some of my troop's events. I look up to my mom because she puts up with me and my aunt, our troop leader, for taking on our Girl Scout troop and teaching us how to be responsible. I also admire my grandmother because she also helps with my scouting. In addition, I can always count on my cousin to listen to me.

I would tell others to keep going and not to give up. Ask your parents for help so you have a support system when things become overwhelming. But, most importantly, I would say believe in yourself and make the right choices. Take time out for other people because the personal reward will be great.

Ashley Zipperer
Jacksonville, FL

Ashley Zipperer is a Jacksonville native born April 27, 1987. She attends Bishop Kenny High School. Service to others has always been an important part of the Zipperers' lives. Her father is a police officer and her mother is a social worker with the Department of Children and Families. Her older brother, who has passed away, taught her to live life to the fullest and not to have any regrets. This has influenced her to do more volunteering and to look for people in need—not only the ones who are asking for help. Ashley is compassionate when it comes to people in need or in trouble, and she is also creative in her ideas of service. Even as a young child, Ashley gave out toys and helped at parties for foster children. In addition to her volunteer work, Ashley enjoys singing with the International Peace Performers and school choir. She likes to hang out with her friends and family on the weekends and is interested in art and the law. Her favorite subjects include religion, humanities, and Spanish.

Special Birthdays

When I was in the seventh grade, my youth group volunteered at an Easter Egg Hunt at the Children's Home Society. Seeing the faces of the children light up made me realize how precious childhood is and that not all children have a happy home life.

From this event and my past experiences with foster children, I knew I needed to do something to make the world a better place, even if it was only for a few children. I always enjoyed the celebration of birthdays with my family and friends. Happy memories are something that will stay with you all your life, and I realized that many children don't have birthday parties. I thought of all the things that made birthdays special and set out to make some children happy. I decided that a monthly birthday party for less-fortunate children would be something I could do.

It seems like a luxury, I know. After all, what does a child need? Food, clothing, a safe shelter, and education, of course, but what about the need to feel special? To be the center of attention? To feel important? Most of us are fortunate enough to look back on our childhood and remember a special day each year where that need was fully met: our birthday.

I began the birthday party project in 2000 at Girls Inc. of Jacksonville, a nonprofit after-school program that provides care for 25 low-income children at its Spring Park Center. I worked with the center director, Virginia Marshall, in setting the date of the party and in determining gifts ideas for the children. The director made me feel like the job I was doing was very important to the children. Each child, during his or her birthday month, is honored at the party. The selection of the theme and the gifts are crucial because I want each person to feel special that day. Decorations, goody bags, and refreshments are served, and everyone has a good time, especially me.

I plan on continuing the parties, and if I am ever unable, I hope that my peers who have come along to the parties are inspired to follow in my footsteps of service.

Many people have helped me with the parties, especially my cousin, Melissa Moberg. She has been an inspiration to me. For example, when I hear that a child is disappointed with his or her present, she says that we did our best. Although I still feel bad, I know there are always obstacles we have to overcome.

I have learned that I can make a difference in the world and stand up to pressures that others can't or won't. I want to be a role model for other youth and let them know that, if I can do it, so can they. I hope that I am setting a good example for others, especially young women, to follow.

I have had many role models in my life, especially my mother. She gives me courage and believes in my dreams. I know she will be there in everything I set out to do. She has helped me become the strong person I am today.

When things are difficult and I feel that I am alone, I am inspired by Anne Frank. She was a person who stood up for what she believed. My favorite quote from her is "How wonderful that no one wait a single moment to start to improve the world." I believe the youth of today are up for the challenge. I know I am.

Many schools require community service, but most kids only do the required number of hours and don't take what they do to heart. My advice to the people who fall into this category is find something you are passionate about and really commit yourself to it. For me, the joy on a child's face when he or she is presented with a gift is so rewarding.

Nicole Zisner
Culver City, CA

Nicole Allyson Zisner was born on September 1, 1987. She lives in Culver City, CA, with her parents, Benjamin and Cindee Zisner; her two brothers, Jonathan and Jeremy; and their English Pug, Pugsly. Nicole attends Culver High School, where her favorite subjects are math, English, and Japanese. She participated in a Japanese immersion program in elementary and middle school and has made two trips to Japan and has hosted several Japanese exchange students. She is a straight-A student in the accelerated academic program and is also an excellent athlete. Her favorite sport is soccer, but she also excels in swimming, camping, backpacking, rock climbing, hiking, and volleyball. She is active in Girl Scouts, and her troop gives much of their free time to community service and charitable work. Nicole's energy and positive attitude have made her one of the most outstanding young women in her community.

Volunteering

I became a Girl Scout when I was 4 years old, as a Daisy, always doing community service. There wasn't much that I could do when I was that young, so I just helped people who I thought needed help. I always enjoyed doing community service wherever I was needed. Our Girl Scout troop adopted a grandmother from the Marina Care Center when we were all 5 years old. She was part of our family for 4 years, until one day when she passed away. It was a sad time for me because I really enjoyed spending time with her. My Daisy troop even bought dinners for families in need for every holiday, and we still do this each year.

Once, in 1999, my mom heard about a young boy with leukemia. I thought it would be a great idea to buy him something he really wanted for Christmas. It was sad when we arrived at his house because there was a note on the door telling us that he was in the hospital again because of a relapse. It touched my heart when he called to thank us from the hospital, crying because he was so happy to receive the Super Nintendo and games for which he had asked. It gives my heart a nice warm feeling of accomplishment knowing that I helped someone who really needed it.

I used to help out my elementary Japanese teacher after school every week while I was in middle school. Then, my mom got me involved in Challenger Little League. I was afraid at first because I wasn't used to being around people who were disabled. After a few games, I realized they were just regular kids like me who also enjoyed a game of T-ball. I became close with one girl, named Michelle Power. She invited me to her 13th birthday party. We have been buddies ever since. Some of the disabled kids used to scare me when I was little, but my mom always taught me to be nice to everyone. Now, I am always excited to see them.

Another thing that I enjoy doing every year is the SIDS Walk. SIDS stands for "Sudden Infant Death Syndrome."

This is always a sad day, but it is my pleasure to help. My favorite part of the day is when we arrive at Veteran's Park after walking six miles. There are speeches and moments of silence to remember the children who died of SIDS. After a few people give their speeches, everyone witnesses a magical sight as doves and monarch butterflies are released. I will always have a wonderful feeling from being part of this celebration.

There wasn't really much to do in preparing for these different functions. I just go and do what I can to help the people who need my assistance. I feel really good knowing that I have helped someone in need. It feels good to be needed! I am sort of shy, but I guess I get the courage to do what I do from my parents. My parents raised me to always help others in any way I can. The Girl Scout Promise also says "On my honor I will try to serve God and my country to help people at all times and to live by the Girl Scout law." The positive part of helping others is they are very happy that I have helped them. I feel great the rest of the day knowing that I have assisted someone. The negatives of volunteering are that sometimes you have to put forth a lot of effort and hard work and, in the end, it does not always turn out the way you had planned. Sometimes, the children I get close to are hospitalized, and it makes me sad to see what some of these kids have to go through every day. It is also difficult when one of the children I have become close with dies.

Something I have learned is that, as long as I am myself, people will like and respect me for who I am. I guess you can say that getting close to someone and having him or her die is a big obstacle. I know that everyone has to die, but why young children? My mother has helped me to be who I am; she, too, likes to help others. She makes friends with so many people and always tries to help them when she can. My mom works with severely disabled people. She advised me to just try helping, and if it was too much, then I wouldn't have to do it anymore. I helped out with Disability Awareness Day with my Girl Scout troop. It was a fun event. I learned some sign language and also saw how blind people have to get around. I also learned about people with cognitive impairments. I really enjoy helping others. Some of my friends would rather go shopping and to the movies. I like to do those things, too, but on Saturdays, I like to help out with Challenger Little League.

I would have to say that my number one female role model is my mother. My mom has so many friends—everyone likes her. She is nice to others and tries to help whoever she can. We don't have a lot of money, but it doesn't take money to be nice to people. She taught me everything I know and teaches me more each day. My mom tells me not to be a quitter. I hope that one day, when I am a mother, I will raise my children the way my mom raised me. She has been the leader of my Girl Scout troop for many years. We are an active troop thanks to her. She encourages and supports me in everything I do. I love her very much, and I know that she will always love me and be there for me. If I had to start my life all over again, I would hope to have the same parents and upbringing so that I could help others.

I also wanted to mention my Grandma Helen. My grandmother has always been a great role model to me. She taught me how to bake, sew, and show love. When I become a grandmother, I will make sure that I always have candy in the house, coloring books, cookies, and ice cream. I will also take my granddaughter to get her nails done. My grandmother has had a tough life. She was in a concentration camp during World War II in Poland. She is a courageous woman who is very special to me.

My advice to others about volunteering is, as long as you are yourself, people will like you. In the end, people will respect you and always remember that you are a good person. Your reward in life will be that you have made at least one person happy.

Meredith Zitron
Cleveland, OH

Meredith Zitron was born on October 22, 1984, in Kansas City, KS, and moved to Cleveland, OH, with her mother, Barbara, in 1987. Meredith attended high school at Hathaway Brown School in Shaker Heights, OH, where she was active in the Israeli Culture Club, the Dance Club, and Gold Key. She was also involved with the Student Research Program, through which she gained several internships with such organizations as History Enterprises and the Cleveland Film Society. Meredith has a strong drive and determination to succeed in everything she does, which is apparent through her internships and other volunteer programs. She is interested in pursuing a career in communications and film and hopes to continue interning and volunteering. Currently, she is a member of the Youth Philanthropy Board at Menorah Park Center for Senior Living and a member on a subcommittee for the Youth Philanthropy and Service project of the Mandel Center at Case Western Reserve University.

Young Philanthropist

My entire life, I have been brought up to be a philanthropic person. The idea of giving donations of money and being generous with my time has been engraved into my head as though it was stone. Whether it is from growing up with a mother who is a fundraiser or amidst the religion of Judaism where it is required to give *tzedakah,* or charitable gifts, there has always been some influence of philanthropy in my life. Although I have been raised with these ideals, it was not until 3 years ago that I really began to evaluate how important it is to be philanthropic.

My involvement with youth philanthropy began when the nonprofit nursing home, Menorah Park Center for Senior Living, in Beachwood, OH, was given a grant to develop a Youth Philanthropy Board. Spearheaded by my mother, who is the development director at the nursing home, the board was created with the purpose of teaching teenagers in the community about philanthropy, values clarification, budgeting, and the grant-making process itself. The establishment of the board was also a chance for either underfunded or overbudget departments to ask for money for a worthwhile project.

The first year I was a member of the board was also the first year of its existence. Given this circumstance, neither the seven other board members nor I knew what to expect. There were some people, like myself, who had some knowledge and familiarity with philanthropy, whereas others had never even heard the word before. We first had to get acquainted with one another and learn about everyone's backgrounds, which eventually helped a great deal when it came time to allocate the $10,000 we had been given among the different departments. Because many of us had never met before, every meeting began with an activity. The activities ranged from exercises that dealt with values clarification, evaluating different aspects of philanthropy, decision-making skills, and, most importantly, getting to know one another.

Although all eight of us were all different individuals, there was one thing we all had in common: Each of us had some kind of connection to the nursing home. This was a prerequisite in order to be a member of the board. We all had to have some kind of association with the nursing home, whether we had volunteered there or had a relative who was an employee or on the board. As time passed, we learned the basics of the grant-making process and what it means to be philanthropic. Soon, it became time to review the grant proposals that were submitted by the various departments.

Reviewing the proposals and the decision-making process in itself was an incredibly stressful and difficult task. It was emotionally tiresome on many of the members, myself in particular. The first step in the allocation process was reviewing all of the proposals that were submitted. After reviewing them, each member was to choose two or three proposals he or she would advocate because he or she believed the project deserved the money. I had chosen two grant proposals, and I was quite confident that both would receive the money. To my disbelief, however, I was overruled and only one of my proposals received the money. I was not quite sure what had gone wrong on my part that only one received the money; but, in the end, I learned from the experience and the decisions that were made. I took the lessons that I learned in persuasion and advocacy to my advantage and applied them in the second year that I was a member of the board.

The second year was new, different, and exciting. The amount of members on the board grew from 8 to 12, and I was one of the veterans. All of the members who were on the board the previous year returned, unless they had graduated. Even from the first meeting in the fall of 2001, I knew in my head that I was going to fight and advocate as hard as I could for my grant proposals. This was not the only difference, however. The largest change was that the amount of money we were given to allocate grew by $10,000. Although we now had $20,000, and it seemed to us like a blessing, there was a downfall to having all of this money. We had requests for twice as much money than we had. As time passed and staff members from various departments came to our meetings to advocate for their departments, it became more apparent which departments really needed the money and which did not. As a result, the decision-making process was not as tedious as it had been the year before.

Most of us agreed with one another, and there was not one person who was completely upset with the decisions. For many of the proposals, half of the money that was requested was granted. It was our thinking that, if we gave many departments half of the money they requested, they could then begin their project, and in the future, if the board saw that the project was successful, the rest of the money would be granted to them. An advantage of allocating the money this way was that, as a board, we were able to distribute the money to many more departments.

At the end of the second year, I was more satisfied with the outcome than I had been the year before. I knew that I had stood up for the departments that I believed in, and I had made sure they were allocated their money. Seeing and hearing their reactions when I told them that they had been given the money was incredibly rewarding and clarified the meaning of philanthropy to me like no other experience. Another rewarding outcome was that I was given the opportunity to be a part of a philanthropy board through Case Western Reserve University.

I am now a member of the Youth Philanthropy and Service Board of the Mandel Center for Nonprofit Organizations at Case Western Reserve University. This philanthropy board, normally referred to as YPS: CHESP, is not specifically designed for The Mandel Center. YPS is the Region 8 Service Learning Collaborative for the state of Ohio. It encourages people in the community to volunteer their time, teach youth about participating in service, and supplies grants for service learning opportunities. Unlike the philanthropy board at Menorah Park, there are two different ways to be involved with YPS. One can either be a part of a subcommittee to teach about the different aspects of philanthropy or be a member of the distribution committee, which allocates money for the actual grant applications.

I am a member of the training subcommittee, which deals with informing different communities about how they can be philanthropic. It is our job to hold training sessions throughout the year, primarily for middle and high school students, to educate them about the various ways philanthropy and service can be performed. Currently, the training committee has been busy planning the first of the training sessions. I am excited to begin sharing my knowledge of philanthropy with others and hopefully teach them something, just as I have been taught.

Teaching and helping others is what philanthropy and service are all about. As a member of these two philanthropy boards, I have been one of the rare teens across the country to partake in such experiences. I am grateful for the opportunities that have been made available to me, and it is my goal this year to commit 110% of myself to these projects. I will forever hold the values and lessons in community service, charity, philanthropy, and giving my time and talent close to my heart and use them whenever possible.

Part 6: Additional Inspiration

*" Having a big heart
has nothing to do with how big your bank account is.
Everyone has something to give. "*

—Barbara Bush

Writing provides a great way to record your goals and accomplishments in donating money, volunteering, and being a positive activist. You can also make a record of the advice you would give to others and the many ways to share it. The following section provides journal pages that will be helpful to you now and in the future. Add other activities as you think of them. Have a great time with your journal.

Why I Want To Make a Difference

You may have many reasons for wanting to make a difference. Feel good about yourself and record your reasons.

1. _____
   _____
   _____
   _____
   _____

2. _____
   _____
   _____
   _____
   _____

3. _____
   _____
   _____
   _____
   _____

4. _____
   _____
   _____
   _____
   _____

5. _____
   _____
   _____
   _____
   _____

My Ideas for Positive Activism

As you look around your school, community, and religious affiliation, there will be specific opportunities to initiate or change many things. What are you going to do that will be positive?

I am committed to positive activism and would like to demonstrate it in several ways.

Place:
- ❏ School
- ❏ Community
- ❏ Religious Affiliation

Goal (s): _____

_____

_____

_____

Objectives	Activities	Date	Accomplishment

Advice to Girls About Positive Activism

Record your advice to others about positive activism.

Positive activism can bring about

_____
_____
_____
_____
_____
_____
_____
_____
_____
_____
_____
_____
_____
_____
_____
_____
_____
_____

The way(s) I'll share my advice on positive activism are:
- ❏ Talk to a friend.
- ❏ Write a story for my school newspaper.
- ❏ Write a story for my hometown newspaper(s).
- ❏ Start a charitable club for girls.
- ❏ Other _____

Log

Name: _____

Date: _____

- ❏ Donating Money
- ❏ Positive Activism
- ❏ Volunteering

Goal Statement: _____

_____

_____

_____

What I would like to accomplish: _____

_____

_____

_____

Accomplishments to date: _____

_____

_____

_____

What I will need to do next: _____

_____

_____

_____

Estimated completion time: _____

_____

_____

Signature: _____

My Ideas for Volunteering and Service Learning

Your school, community, and religious affiliation offer many opportunities for volunteering and service learning.

I like volunteering because: _____

_____

_____

_____

_____

_____

What I have accomplished in volunteering:

Name of Organization	Responsibilities	Number of Hours

How I Feel About Myself
When I Volunteer

Record information regarding the way(s) you have given of your time, where, what you did, and how you feel about volunteering.

Where I Have Volunteered _____

_____

_____

_____

_____

_____

What I Accomplished _____

_____

_____

_____

_____

_____

Number of Hours Given _____

_____

_____

_____

_____

_____

How I Feel About Myself When I Volunteer _____

_____

_____

_____

_____

_____

Advice to Girls About Volunteering

Through your own experiences in volunteering, what advice would you give to others? Write your top three pieces of advice about being a volunteer.

1. _____
   _____
   _____
   _____
   _____

2. _____
   _____
   _____
   _____
   _____

3. _____
   _____
   _____
   _____
   _____

How will you share your advice on volunteering with others?
- ❑ Talk to a friend.
- ❑ Write a story for my school newspaper.
- ❑ Write a story for my hometown newspaper(s).
- ❑ Write a story for a magazine.
- ❑ Appear on a TV talk show.
- ❑ Other _____

Ideas for Donating Money

Perhaps you have money from doing household chores, babysitting, or it may have been given to you for special occasions such as a birthday or holiday. Some students set aside money to donate to charities and organizations. How might you donate your money?

I would like to donate money and will consider the following charities and groups:

Charity/Group	Reason for Selection	Amount to be Given	Date for Donation

How I Feel About Myself
When I Donate Money

Record information regarding the money you have given, the charity/group receiving it, how the money was used, and how you feel about yourself because of your donation.

- Amount of Money Given _____

_____

_____

_____

_____

_____

- The Charity/Group Receiving the Money _____

_____

_____

_____

_____

_____

- How the Money Was Used_____

_____

_____

_____

_____

_____

- How I Feel About Myself for Donating the Money

_____

_____

_____

_____

_____

Advice to Other Girls
About Giving Money

My advice to others about giving money is _____

_____

_____

_____

_____

_____

_____

_____

_____

_____

_____

_____

_____

_____

_____

_____

_____

_____

_____

_____

The way(s) I'll share my advice on giving money are:

❑ Talk to a friend.
❑ Write a story for my school newspaper.
❑ Write a story for my hometown newspaper(s).
❑ Start a charitable club for girls.
❑ Other_____

My Plan for Achieving My Goals

Developing a schedule for success is important for the completion of your goals. Keep a record of everything you do. You may want to put this on your computer.

Days of the Week	Task(s) to be Completed
Monday	
Tuesday	
Wednesday	
Thursday	
Friday	
Saturday	
Sunday	

Ways to Inform Others About
Your Charitable Actions

- Talk with friends and encourage them to donate money to charities and other groups.
- Write an article for your school newspaper.
- Write a letter to the editors of your local and weekly newspapers.
- Interview other girls about their charitable acts and share their stories in as many ways as possible.
- Write a slogan for a bumper sticker.
- Create a video documentary on your accomplishments.
- Create a poster and ask permission to display it in your classroom, a prominent place in your school, in a local business, or in your public library.
- Write a public service announcement for local radio stations and TV cable channels.
- Create a Web site for girls on donating money, positive activism, and volunteering.
- Establish a school or community club for girls to assist them in understanding the value of being charitable.

What I Have Learned About Myself

Through your various charitable activities, you will learn more about yourself. As you discover certain abilities, use this form to record them.

Abilities: _____

_____

_____

Interests: _____

_____

Attitudes: _____

_____

Work Habits: _____

_____

Time Management Strengths: _____

_____

_____

Planning Abilities: _____

_____

Interpersonal Skills: _____

_____

Empathy: _____

_____

Working with Groups: _____

_____

Hall of Fame
Nomination Form

There are millions of girls and women who have contributed money, volunteered, or been a positive activist. Nominate your choices for the hall of fame.

Nominee	Reason for Nomination

My Favorite Books

There are great books about philanthropy, volunteering, and positive activism. What are your favorite books on these topics and why do you like them?

Title: _____

Author: _____

Why I like this book: _____

_____

_____

_____

Title: _____

Author: _____

Why I like this book: _____

_____

_____

_____

Title: _____

Author: _____

Why I like this book: _____

_____

_____

_____

Title: _____

Author: _____

Why I like this book: _____

_____

_____

_____

Timeline of Female Giving

Women have donated money, securities, and property for a variety of purposes including the arts, medicine, education, disabilities, community needs, and religion. A few examples follow.

1871 Sophia Smith donated $393,105 to establish Smith College.

1887 Josephine Louise LeMonnier Newcomb donated $100,000 to establish H. Sophie Newcomb Memorial College of Tulane University.

1928 Anna M. Richardson Harkness left $20 million to establish the Commonwealth Fund. She also left many other gifts to other institutions.

1983 Lucy Goldschmidt Moses gave $5 million to Jewish Philanthropies of New York.

1989 Clare Booth Luce donated $70 million of her estate for science education for undergraduate women.

1992 Helen Copley donated $2.5 million to the San Diego Symphony Orchestra.

1993 Cindy Crawford donated more than $70,000 to the University of Wisconsin Children's Hospital.

1993 Barbara Streisand donated her Malibu ranch, valued at $15 million, to Santa Monica Mountains Conservancy.

1994 Harriet Bullitt and Patsy Bullitt Collins declared they would give almost all of their estate, worth $375 million, to causes concerning the environment.

1994 Joan Kroc gave $80 million to the Salvation Army.

1994 Joan Tisch gave $1 million to the United Jewish Appeal Federation AIDS Initiative.

1995 Sallie Bingham gave $10 million to establish the Kentucky Foundation for Women and $3.5 million to Santa Fe Stages to help a new theater group company and its film festival.

1995 Mariah Carey donated $1 million to create Camp Mariah for the Fresh Air Fund.

1995 Teresa Heinz donated $36 million for a grant to support the Heinz Awards.

1995 Osceola McCarty donated $150,000 for scholarships at The University of Southern Mississippi.

1996 Lillian Bounds Disney gave $100,000 to the Nez Perce Indian Reservation.

1997 Eleanor Boyer gave her New Jersey lottery winnings of approximately $8 million to local nonprofit organizations and her church.

1997 Enid Smith Goodrich left the following: $40 million to the Children's Museum in Indianapolis, $80 million to the Liberty Fund, and $40 million to the Indianapolis Museum of Art.

1997 Gladys Holm left $18 million to the Children's Memorial Hospital in Chicago.

1997 Joan B. Kroc donated $15 million for recovery efforts from the 1997 spring flood to the citizens of Grand Forks, ND.

1997 Dolly Parton donated $100,000 to Sanders Sevier Medical Center for the building of a birth center.

1999 Audrey Beck donated 47 paintings to the Museum of Fine Arts in Houston, adding to the 23 works that had already been donated. All 70 paintings are estimated to be worth $150–200 million.

1999 Margaret R. Bradshaw gave $2 million to the Wellness Center at Memorial Hermann Healthcare System.

1999 Hazel M. Crismon left $1 million to the Guide Dog Foundation for the Blind.

1999 Gertrude Donnelly Hess gave $1.25 million for a cancer research professorship at Case Western Reserve University.

1999 Catherine Stewart Jones left $8.5 million to the Community Foundation of Central Georgia.

1999 Kathleen (Katsy) Mason left $1.35 million for the Grand Canyon Trust.

1999 Pleasant Rowland gave $5 million to establish a visitor's center and a new garden at Chicago Botanic Garden.

2000 Gratia (Topsy) Montgomery donated $8 million to build two research vessels at the Woods Hole Oceanographic Institute.

2001 Anne C. Anderson donated $33.4 million at the time of her death for hospital teaching activities and programs, as well as $1.5 million during her life for a chair in Surgery at the Lehigh Valley Hospital and Health Network.

2001 Deborah A. Bricker and Kelly A. Rosen gave $1 million to Goodman Theater to start a children's program.

2001 Iva M. Hargett left $1.2 million to establish the Friends of Hamilton School's Foundation which will provide scholarships to Hamilton High School students who plan to attend college.

2001 Fern McAlister made a $38.3 million bequest for research at the Children's Hospital Los Angeles.

2001 Sarah H. Sayler gave $3.3 million to the League of People With Disabilities.

2001 Irma C. Sprinkle gave $1.3 million to create a scholarship at Hampden-Sydney College.

2002 Marcia L. Hubbard left $4 million to Lancaster Country Day School.

2002 Meg Whitman gave $30 million for a new residential college at Princeton University.

Additional Inspirational Quotes

"If you want happiness for a lifetime, help someone else."
—Chinese Proverb

"It's easy to make a buck. It's a lot tougher to make a difference."
—Tom Brokaw

"Through community volunteerism, young people can gain experiences that build leadership skills—the ability to realize a vision, engage and develop others, and make things happen. "
—Thomas A. Page
President and CEO, San Diego Gas & Electric

"It is in giving oneself that one receives."
—St. Francis of Assisi

"Great opportunities to help others seldom come, but small ones surround us every day."
—Sally Koch

"There is no greater commitment than when people give of themselves. Volunteer activity is the ultimate demonstration of caring."
—John W. Amerman
Chairman of the Board, Mattel, Inc.

"When you cease to make a contribution, you begin to die."
—Eleanor Roosevelt

"We have an obligation to give something back to the communities that give us so much."
—Ray Kroc

"If you can dream it, you can do it."
—Walt Disney